ON STAGE

Theater Games and Activities for Kids

SECOND EDITION

Lisa Bany-Winters

CHICAGO
REVIEW
PRESS

Copyright © 1997, 2012 by Lisa Bany-Winters
Second edition
Published by Chicago Review Press, Incorporated
814 North Franklin Street
Chicago, Illinois 60610

ISBN 978-1-61374-073-6

Cover and interior design: Sarah Olson
Cover and interior illustrations: Jim Spence

Library of Congress Cataloging-in-Publication Data
Bany-Winters, Lisa.
  On stage : theater games and activities for kids / Lisa Bany-Winters. — 2nd ed.
     p. cm.
  Includes bibliographical references.
  ISBN 978-1-61374-073-6 (pbk.)
 1. Drama in education. 2. Play. 3. Children's plays, American. I. Title.

PN3171.B27 2012
372.66'044—dc23

2012012741

Printed in the United States of America
5 4 3 2 1

To Michaela and Carlin with love

Contents

Introduction

Acting and theater games help people of all ages focus and concentrate their energies and improve their writing and communication skills, which are useful tools in every aspect of life. *On Stage* is a book designed to help children learn by doing. They can expand their imaginations, free the way they think, talk, and move. They'll learn how to express themselves with their voices and their bodies.

Theater skills enhance children's self esteem, make it easier to step into new situations, help them problem-solve, strengthen listening skills, encourage cooperation, make interaction with others more comfortable, and manage public speaking fears. Although this book is recommended for children between the ages of six and twelve, children as young as four or five can understand the basic acting concepts in these pages. And anyone who is young at

heart will have fun with these theater games and improvisation activities.

The serious performer, director, and drama teacher will find that all acting techniques can be taught through games, which can foster a variety of performance, storytelling, and character-development skills. Games at the beginning of a class or rehearsal strengthen work with a script by helping actors warm up, focus their energy, develop their characters, work with each other, and even memorize their lines.

Most of these games require few props and little or no advance preparation. Many games can be changed for more fun. Some ideas are listed following many of the activities. These sections are called "Play It Again, Sam!" The first chapter of this book, "Getting Onstage," includes fun ways to teach some very important theater terms and basic theater concepts, such as blocking and stage pictures. These terms will be of special interest to teachers or directors working with young children. The exercises in this chapter are excellent for early rehearsals or drama classes because they give performers the foundation for communicating throughout rehearsals and classes.

The second chapter, "Twisting Your Tongue and Warming Up," includes games that are great to do at the beginning of class or rehearsal or before a show to help young people prepare physically and vocally for performing.

The third chapter, "Anytime Theater Games," is filled with games that are great for enhancing listening skills and fostering cooperation. Some of these games can also serve as ice breakers for students who are shy.

The fourth chapter, "Theater in the Round (Games Played in a Circle)," offers games that work well with groups. They can be played standing or sitting in a circle. They make good party games or can be used as actor warm-ups. These games help strengthen improvisation, memorization, and focusing skills as well as promote team building.

Chapter 5, "Make 'Em Laugh (Ideas for Funny Scenes)," will give children a chance to develop their comedic skills. Creative writing teachers might find these activities useful because they help participants develop story lines and flesh out characters.

The sixth chapter, "Creating Characters," will help children further flesh out their characters by letting them explore how a character walks, talks, thinks, eats, and everything else that makes a character unique.

"Improvisation" is the title and focus of the seventh chapter. Here's where young actors can develop their thinking and doing skills in an environment where anything can happen. Because there are no props or scenery, you can create anything simply by saying it.

Chapter 8 is precisely titled "Using and Becoming Objects" because students are given the opportunity to become inanimate objects, like a chair, a hat, or a rug. They can also find new, creative uses for familiar objects.

"Creative Drama," the ninth chapter, shows how to use pantomime, puppets, or masks to tell a story onstage.

In the tenth chapter, called "Behind the Scenes," young actors will learn what goes on behind the scenes and offstage at every theatrical production. Readers will be introduced to the people who help make the magic onstage, including the sound-effects technician, costume designer, makeup artist, and prop master.

The final chapter, "Monologues, Scenes, and Plays," provides a few examples of children's performance pieces that are ready to be used.

You can teach these chapters in order or in any order you want. The point is to make as much fun as you can in whatever time you have available. And remember, the magic of theater can happen on a stage, in a yard, or in a classroom. All you need is your imagination and the desire to have fun.

★ 1

Getting Onstage

This chapter is about basic theater words, and it also has games to help you learn them. The words in quotation marks in this chapter, such as "blocking" and "cross," are used by professional actors and actresses in plays on Broadway, in your hometown theaters, and around the world. These words help the cast and crew talk to each other about their jobs. You can use them when you put on plays at school, in your home, or anywhere else.

You can practice your theater knowledge with the games in this chapter. **Blocking** and **Upstage Downstage** are games that explain the basics of movement onstage (which means the part of the stage that is visible to an audience, as opposed to "off-stage," which is the part of a stage that is not visible and lies behind the scenes). **Stage**

Picture reminds you to never turn your back to the audience. **The Directing Game** puts you in the director's chair, and **Who's Who in Theater** explains everybody's important role in creating and performing a play.

You don't need a stage for theater games. Just pick an open space and decide where the (pretend) audience is sitting. *Poof*—instant stage! For example, if you're in your backyard, the audience can be where the door to your house is, and if you're in your classroom, the audience can be the desks.

And now, let's get onstage and discover the magic of theater.

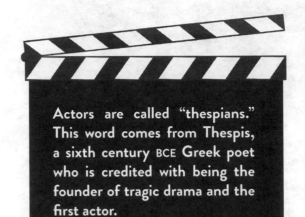

Actors are called "thespians." This word comes from Thespis, a sixth century BCE Greek poet who is credited with being the founder of tragic drama and the first actor.

Blocking

"**B**locking" means where you stand and how you move onstage. "Stage directions" tell you where to go.

"Upstage" is the area on the stage that is furthest from the audience. "Downstage" is the area closest to the audience. "Stage right" is the actor's right, not the audience's. "Stage left" is the actor's left. "Center stage" is in the middle.

Why is it called "upstage" and "downstage"? In the nineteenth century and earlier, theaters had "raked"—or sloped—stages. That means upstage was actually higher than downstage, and the stage slanted down as it got closer to the audience. This made it easier for the audience to see everyone onstage.

In theater, the word "cross" means to walk to a place on the stage. For example, you might say, "Cross the street," while a director might say, "Cross to stage left." In a script, stage directions are usually written within parentheses and italicized or written on the right side of the page. Actors don't read them out loud, but they follow the stage direction instructions. For example, the script might read:

> ALICE:
>
>> I wonder what will happen if I drink this.
>> (Drinks from the bottle and grows taller.)

However, the actor portraying Alice says, "I wonder what will happen if I drink this," and then performs the action described in parentheses.

Stage directions can be written in the script, or you can get them from the director of the play. The director is in charge of the actors' movement onstage. The director also gets to cast the play. This mean he or she gets to decide who will play each part.

A stage direction or director might say, "Cross from downstage left to upstage right." See if you can do this without turning your back to the audience.

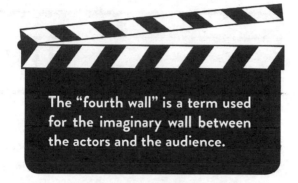

The "fourth wall" is a term used for the imaginary wall between the actors and the audience.

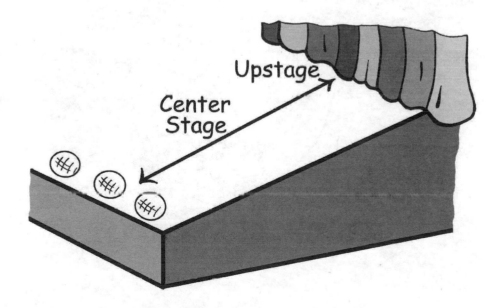

Upstage

Center Stage

Upstage Downstage

Two or more actors

earning stage directions is an important first step to staging a play. Here's a great way to learn them so you can understand where to go onstage.

This game is best played on a stage. If a stage is not available, chose a large space and decide where the audience or downstage is located.

PROPS

★ Paper
★ Pen or pencil
★ Hat (or a bowl if you don't have a hat)

Write the following stage directions on nine separate pieces of paper:

★ Upstage right
★ Upstage center
★ Upstage left
★ Center stage right
★ Center stage
★ Center stage left
★ Downstage right
★ Downstage center
★ Downstage left

Fold each piece of paper and place them all in the hat. Choose one player to be the director. The director pulls out a stage direction from the hat. She reads aloud whatever stage direction she has pulled out of the hat, and all the other players must quickly move to the area that the director calls. For example, if the direction is upstage right, everyone must go to the back of the stage and to the right side when facing the audience. Then the director pulls out another stage direction and says, "Cross to . . . ," then says the stage direction chosen. The other players cross or walk to that area of the stage, and the game continues from there.

After a few turns, let someone else be the director.

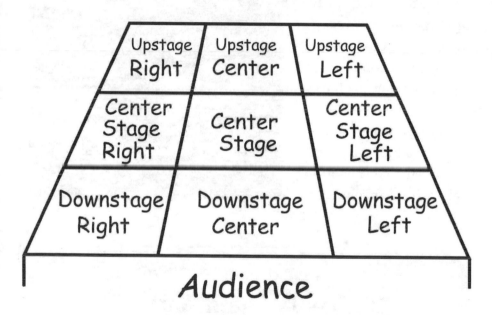

 Play It Again, Sam!

Think of other stage directions to add, such as:

★ Face stage right and point with your upstage hand (the hand furthest from the audience)
★ Cross center stage and kneel on your downstage knee
★ Cross downstage left hopping on your upstage foot
★ Cross upstage center while facing downstage right
★ Pat someone on the back using your upstage hand

The director can make the stage direction for only some of the people by saying, "Everyone wearing blue cross to . . . ," or "Everyone who ate cereal for breakfast cross to . . ." When you're playing with a group, see who can complete each stage direction first. See how many special stage directions you can come up with and add them to the hat.

Stage Picture

Three or more actors

This game is best played on a stage. If a stage is not available, chose a large space and decide where the audience is seated.

During a play, if the audience clearly can see everything, that means the performers have created a "good stage picture." It's very important to face the audience and to make sure the audience can see everyone onstage. If you are blocking someone from being seen or if someone is blocking you, that's called "upstaging." The important things to remember in this game are

1. Face the audience;

2. Don't upstage anyone; and

3. Don't let anyone upstage you.

Choose one player to be the director. The director tells everyone to walk around. The other players walk around the stage, going wherever they want but staying where the audience can see them. At any time the director calls out, "Stage picture!" and everyone must immediately freeze and strike a pose in a good stage picture. The director can move from side to side in the "house" (which is where the audience sits) to make sure it is a good stage picture from any and every angle.

You are out of the game if, when the director calls "Stage picture," you (a) have your back to the audience, (b) are upstaging someone, or (c) are being upstaged by someone. You must leave the stage. But then you can help the director decide who's out. When he's ready, the director says, "Walk around," and the game continues.

Acting tip for making a good stage picture: If you're downstage (see **Upstage Downstage**), you may want to kneel down so you don't upstage anyone behind you. And, if you're upstage, you may want to strike a nice tall pose (but be sure you're not right behind anyone).

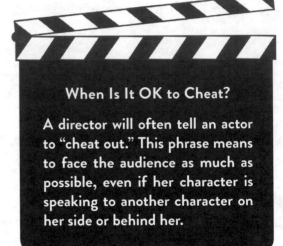

When Is It OK to Cheat?

A director will often tell an actor to "cheat out." This phrase means to face the audience as much as possible, even if her character is speaking to another character on her side or behind her.

 Play It Again, Sam!

Add more rules to make the game more difficult. For example, you can tell all players that their poses must be big and dramatic and that everyone must smile.

The Directing Game

Three or more actors

One of a director's jobs is to give the actors ideas for how to say their lines and how to move onstage. This game lets you do just that.

PROP

★ A chair

Pick one person to be the director and have her sit in the director's chair. Everyone else makes up a short scene—one that includes a lot of action. Here's one example:

Two kids are playing in the park, when all of the sudden there is an explosion. The kids faint. Another person screams and runs to get the firefighters. The firefighters come in, put out the fire, and wake the kids.

Once the scene has been created, the director calls out, "Places!" This means everyone goes to his or her place for the beginning of the scene. Then the director calls out, "Action!" and the scene begins. The actors go through the entire short scene, and when the scene is over, the director calls out, "Cut!"

Next, the director assigns each actor a direction, such as, "Slow motion." The director then calls out, "Places!" Once everyone is in

place, she calls out, "Action!" and the actors begin acting out the same scene. But this time, they do it in slow motion. The actors continue to perform the scene until the director yells, "Cut!"

The director also can assign two directions at once, such as, "Slow motion, opera style." The actors act out the same scene in slow motion, and instead of speaking or making regular sounds, they sing like opera singers—even for the fire engine or police siren!

The director can even assign three directions at once, such as, "Slow motion, opera style, while pretending to hula hoop." It doesn't take much to make this a wild and crazy game!

The "intermission" is the break between the acts of a play. During intermission, the audience can stretch their legs or get a bite to eat while the cast and crew prepare for the next act. It's like halftime at a football game. Intermissions started when theaters were lit by candles. The candles had to be trimmed after an hour or so.

SUGGESTIONS FOR OTHER DIRECTIONS

★ Fast-forward

★ Overdramatic

★ Doing the chicken dance

★ Walking through Jell-O

★ Laughing hysterically

★ On one foot

★ Under water

★ Very nervous

★ Backward

You can think of a lot more!

Who's Who in Theater

From the first idea for a play to the final applause, there are all sorts of important jobs involved in creating theater. Each job is important and must be completed to create a successful performance. (We'll explore most of these jobs in more detail in chapter 10, "Behind the Scenes.") Here's the rundown on who helps the curtain go up.

Producer: The producer is in charge of the business part of theater. He or she hires the staff and manages all the money, which means paying the staff and making sure tickets are sold. To sell tickets, a producer might advertise in a newspaper or online and make posters for the play.

Director: The director is in charge of all onstage movement other than dancing. He or she casts the show and blocks the play. The director will coach the actors in developing their characters in the beginning of the rehearsal process, and he or she will also give them notes about how to improve the play during later rehearsals.

Actor: Actors are the performers. They memorize their lines and develop their characters. They also get to take bows (called "curtain calls") and get a lot of applause for their contribution to a play production. Boys and girls can both be called "actors." (It's easier than saying "actors" and "actresses" all the time, and it makes everyone equal.)

Choreographer: The choreographer stages all of the dances in the play. He or she works with the director and musical director to make sure the dances will work well in the production; then the choreographer teaches the dances to the actors.

Musical Director: The musical director works with the director and choreographer to see that the music in the play fits in with the acting and the dancing. He or she helps the actors learn the songs for the play and gives them musical instruction. The musical director is also in charge of the musicians.

Stage Manager: The stage manager helps the director during rehearsals. He or she writes down the blocking so there is a plan of movement on paper and so that everyone can remember it. The stage manager writes

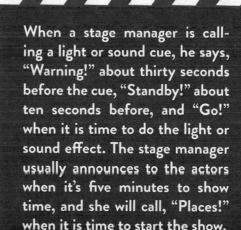

When a stage manager is calling a light or sound cue, he says, "Warning!" about thirty seconds before the cue, "Standby!" about ten seconds before, and "Go!" when it is time to do the light or sound effect. The stage manager usually announces to the actors when it's five minutes to show time, and she will call, "Places!" when it is time to start the show.

up the rehearsal schedule, makes sure the rehearsal space is set up for rehearsals, checks all the lighting and sound equipment to make sure it's in working order, and makes certain that anything the actors or director need is available. During performances, the stage manager calls the show. "Calling the show" means telling the light and sound-board operators (see "crew") when to fade or bring up the lights and sound throughout the performance. The stage manager is like a police officer who directs traffic backstage.

Designer: There are different types of designers. Some designers make the sets, costumes, lighting, sound, props, and makeup. First, the designers meet with the director to come up with ways to make a show look and sound just right. Then they design or create their part of the show.

★ The set designer creates the scenery—the background or setting for the play.

★ The costume designer is responsible for what the actors wear. Costumes are important to help recreate the look of the time period. For example, if the play takes place in a castle in the 1800s, it wouldn't be right for the actors to wear gym shoes.

★ The lighting designer creates the lighting, which can set the mood or let the audience know what time of day it is.

★ The sound designer is in charge of any sound effects or recorded music needed for the play. Perhaps the play takes place on a stormy night. The lighting designer could make the stage look like nighttime, and the sound designer could create the sounds of the storm.

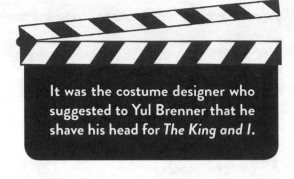

It was the costume designer who suggested to Yul Brenner that he shave his head for *The King and I.*

★ The properties (or "props") designer, sometimes called a props master, is in charge of getting or making any items carried on the stage by actors. For example, in *The Wizard of Oz*, the witch's broomstick is her prop because she carries it.

★ The makeup designer makes the actors' faces look like their characters. For example, by wearing stage makeup, young people can be made to look very old. You can also become animals or other characters with the help of makeup.

Crew: During performances, the crew has a number of important jobs. The stage crew changes the set in between scenes, the light-board operator fades the lights up and down, and the sound-board operator runs the music or sound effects. There might also be a spot-light or follow-spot operator who shines a spot light on the actor who is speaking. These people are usually in the light booth, where the light and sound boards are located.

Understudy: The understudy is like a substitute actor. He or she learns specific parts so that, if an actor gets sick or cannot perform for whatever reason, the understudy can replace the actor.

Twisting Your Tongue and Warming Up

Just like athletes warm up before a game, actors warm up before performing. But they don't just warm up their bodies—they warm up their voices, too. It's very important that the audience understand every word an actor says so they can follow the plot (story) that is being told onstage. Practice speaking loud and clear and enunciating every word. "Enunciating" means pronouncing or clearly saying every syllable and consonant.

This chapter is full of fun warm-ups—some for your body, some for your voice, and some for both!

You can try out **Tongue Twisters** with your friends or parents. Practice them and see how fast you can say them. Then warm up by shaking it all out with **Father Abraham**, a song that uses the body as well as the voice.

Energy Ball is an especially good transition game for those times when you need a fun, quiet thing to do. You can pass the energy ball around while waiting in the doctor's office or backstage before your show begins.

Mirrors is a focus activity that gets players concentrating. **The Number Game** is a focusing and listening game. It's a challenging game for people of all ages.

Warming up and concentrating on one part of the body at a time is called "isolation." The **Isolations** activity is a great way to stretch out and relax from head to toe. Actors warm up their bodies so that they will be ready to make their bodies become different characters or move freely—whatever a script demands.

Echo helps you learn about projection, which means to speak loudly. This is an important skill for the theater, because the audience always needs to be able to hear and understand you.

Character of the Space is a way to get used to the space you're working in and help you get focused at the same time. In this game, you'll explore your environment while concentrating on different ways to move your body.

Space Walk, **Silent Disco Dance Party**, **Attention!**, **Little Sally Walker**, and **Show Us How to Get Down!** let kids express themselves through their own kind of dance. **Great Minds** will show how wonderful it is when "great minds think alike.

Once you warm up with a few of these activities, you'll be ready to get down to the serious work—and fun—of acting.

Tongue Twisters

One or more actors

For stretching out your mouth and getting ready to speak in front of an audience, actors use tongue twisters to warm up. Try the tongue twisters in this activity. As you get better at them, try saying them faster and faster. Think of some tongue twisters of your own.

Start by saying this phrase ten times in a row:

You can find a lot of great tongue twisters in Dr. Seuss books, such as *Oh Say Can You Say* and *Dr. Seuss's ABC.*

Unique New York

Repeat this phrase five times (be sure to pronounce the consonants like the *d* sound in "red," the *p* sound in "copper," and the *t* sound in "kettle," "brittle," and "brattle"):

Red leather, yellow leather, copper kettle, brittle brattle, scadadilly dee (clap), *scadadilly doo* (clap).

Repeat this one five times. Then repeat it five more times while snapping your fingers along with the rhythm.

A knapsack strap, the strap of a knapsack

Try repeating this one five times:

The big black bug bit the big brown bear and the big brown bear bled blood.

Here's a new twist on an old favorite. Be sure to enunciate every *p.*

Peter Piper, the pickled-pepper picker, picked a peck of pickled peppers

A peck of pickled peppers did Peter Piper, the pickled-pepper picker, pick

If Peter Piper, the pickled-pepper picker, picked a peck of pickled peppers

Then where is the peck of pickled peppers that Peter Piper, the pickled-pepper picker, picked?

The following sentence is for practicing projection. Take a deep breath and hold each *o* sound. Pretend you're talking to someone across the sea, but don't strain your voice. Support it with your breath.

Those old boats don't float.

Try repeating this one ten times:

Aluminum linoleum

For the next phrase, overenunciate each word, exercising the part of the mouth you are talking about:

The lips, the teeth, the tip of the tongue

Be sure to say "whether" and "weather" differently in this one:

Whether the weather is cold
Whether the weather is hot
We'll weather the weather, whatever the weather
Whether we like it or not

Once you get good at this one, try bouncing a ball as you say it:

A skunk sat on a stump
The skunk thought the stump stunk
The stump thought the skunk stunk
Which stunk, the skunk or the stump?

Father Abraham

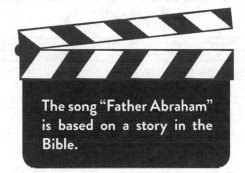

The song "Father Abraham" is based on a story in the Bible.

One or more actors

Singing is a great way to warm up your voice. This song also warms up your body. That's why it's the perfect warm-up for just before a performance. Be sure to sing loud and clear and move your body, too.

> *Father Abraham had seven sons, and*
> *Seven sons had Father Abraham.*
> *And they never laughed, and they never cried.*
> *All they did was go like this*
> *With a left.*

Shake your left hand. Keep shaking it while continuing to sing.

> *Father Abraham had seven sons, and*
> *Seven sons had Father Abraham.*
> *And they never laughed, and they never cried.*
> *All they did was go like this.*
> *With a left,*

Shake your left hand.

> *And a right.*

Shake your right hand. Continue shaking both hands while continuing to sing.

> *Father Abraham had seven sons and*
> *Seven sons had Father Abraham.*
> *And they never laughed, and they never cried.*
> *All they did was go like this.*
> *With a left,*

Shake your left hand.

> *And a right.*

Shake your right hand.

> *And a left.*

Shake your left foot. Keep shaking both hands and your left foot while continuing to sing.

> *Father Abraham had seven sons, and*
> *Seven sons had Father Abraham.*
> *And they never laughed, and they never cried.*
> *All they did was go like this.*
> *With a left,*

Shake your left hand.

And a right.

Shake your right hand.

And a left.

Shake your left foot.

And a right.

Shake your right foot. Keep shaking both hands and feet* while continuing to sing.

> *Father Abraham had seven sons, and*
> *Seven sons had Father Abraham.*
> *And they never laughed, and they never cried.*
> *All they did was go like that.*

---

* To shake both feet without falling down, switch off feet—shake your left foot, hop on your left foot to shake your right foot, hop on your right foot to shake your left foot, and so on. Do it quickly to get the best warm-up.

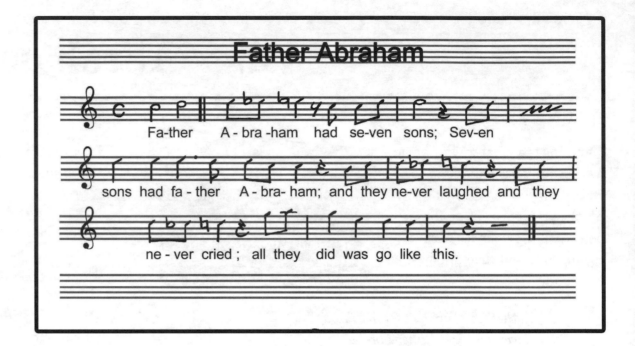

Energy Ball

Two or more actors

I'VE GOT THE ENERGY BALL!

The curtain will go up in five minutes. You're backstage in costume and makeup, ready to go on. You're nervous and excited, but you have to be quiet because you don't want the audience to hear you. You can focus all that energy by playing this game using an imaginary ball of energy.

Hold your hands up in front of you with your palms out. When you have the energy ball, your fingers must tingle and move quickly, like you are waving to someone. But your hands should look like they are holding a ball while you do this.

Then look at someone else. Make eye contact with him and toss the energy ball to him. It should look just like you are tossing a real ball. Now his fingers are tingling and moving quickly around the ball until he tosses it to someone else.

Toss the energy ball around and see if you can always tell who has it. When you get good at it, try tossing two energy balls around. When you get *really* good at it, you can even play energy volleyball.

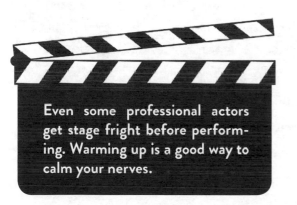

Even some professional actors get stage fright before performing. Warming up is a good way to calm your nerves.

Play It Again, Sam!

Start the game with everyone making a circle, eyes closed, stretching out their hands, tingling their fingers all together, and creating a big imaginary energy ball in the center. Think of sending all of your energy into the ball. Then someone picks up the imaginary ball and begins tossing it around.

Play **Break a Leg Energy Ball**. Concentrate on sending good wishes into the ball, like the wish that everyone has a great show. Then, as the ball is tossed around, think of it as if it is carrying this "good luck" message to each person.

Mirrors

Two
or more
actors

Mirrors is a focus warm-up. It is a quiet game that requires a great deal of concentration.

Everyone chooses a partner. Each pair needs to decide who is player A and who is player B. Stand facing each other, about two feet apart, and make eye contact. Begin with player A as the mover and player B as the mirror. Player A should make slow movements with his arms, legs, torso, and face. While keeping constant eye contact with player A, player B acts like his reflection in a mirror, doing exactly what he does at the exact same time. But player B can't look at the body part of player A that is moving—players must maintain eye contact throughout this exercise.

After a few minutes, player A says, "Switch." Without stopping, player B takes over as the leader of the movement and player A becomes the mirror. After a few minutes, the new leader A can say, "Switch," and the roles are reversed once again. Do this back and forth a few times, giving each player a chance to be the mirror.

In productions of *Snow White and the Seven Dwarves*, the magic mirror is often played by someone speaking offstage.

 Play It Again, Sam!

Play **Guess Who's the Mirror**. Someone goes out of the room while players choose who is player A and who is player B. Begin mirroring. When the person sent out of the room reenters, she will guess which player is the mover and which is the mirror. Even when you say "Switch," the change should be so smooth that it is very hard for anyone to guess.

The Number Game

Four or more actors

Listening is an important skill for actors. They must hear what the other actors are saying in order to respond naturally, and they must listen to their director. It's easy to get distracted and start to think about other things. **The Number Game** helps actors develop their listening skills and helps them stay focused. Because you improve at this game the more you play, you may want to consistently start your rehearsals with this game. You may also want to put a time limit on how long you play, because once you get started, it's hard to stop.

Everyone stands in a circle and counts off, remembering their number. The last person always begins, so if there are six people, number six begins by saying someone else's number ("Four," for example). Number four then calls out someone else's number ("Two," for example). Number two calls out another number, and so on. When you hear your number, say someone else's number.

Sound easy? Wait, here are the rules:

"I'll probably come out onstage, take one look at those three-eyed TV monsters and faint dead away." —Judy Garland, describing her stage fright for her first television appearance in 1955

RULES:

1. No pausing. As soon as you hear your number, say another number. If you wait too long, you're out.

2. Don't say your own number. If you do, you're out.

3. Don't say a number that nobody has. For example, if there are six people playing and you call out, "Seven," you're out.

4. When you're out, you go to the last place in the circle and become the last number. Everyone else gets to move up one number. Again, the last person (that's you now) starts. The game gets tricky because everyone has to remember their new number and can't say their own number.

Here's an example. Let's say six people are playing: Lisa (one), Danny (two), Stephanie (three), Joe (four), Susie (five), and Brian (six). The game begins with Brian calling out, "Number two." Danny quickly calls out, "Number two." Danny gets out because when Brian called his number, he quickly called out his own number. So he moves to the end of the circle and becomes number six. Stephanie, Joe, Susie, and Brian move up one number (because they were behind Danny), but Lisa keeps the same number (because she was in front of Danny). The new order is: Lisa (one), Stephanie (two), Joe (three), Susie (four), Brian (five) and Danny (six). The game begins again with Danny calling out, "Number four."

Play It Again, Sam!

When you get good at playing **The Number Game**, it's time to add on. You can add on just about any kind of thing you like, such as ice-cream flavors. Everyone chooses a different ice-cream flavor, says it out loud, and remembers it. Now start the game again, only this time you can say someone else's number or ice-cream flavor. For example, you may be number three and rocky road. If anyone calls out, "Rocky road," you say someone else's ice-cream flavor or number. But you must do it quickly, and you can't say your own! When someone gets out, she still becomes the last number, and the people who were after that player move up in number but keep the same ice-cream flavor. Flavors don't change. So now you might be number two, but you are still rocky road.

Next, you can add on something else in order, such as days of the week. Number one becomes Monday, number two is Tuesday, and so on. Now you have a number, an ice-cream flavor, and a day of the week. You can call out any one of these things, but don't call out your own! If you get out, numbers and days of the week change, but ice-cream flavors don't change. You can continue to add on—switching off between things that stay the same and things that have an order—and change when someone gets out.

SUGGESTIONS FOR ADD-ONS THAT STAY WITH YOU

★ Sound and movement
★ Colors
★ Cars
★ Countries
★ Lunch meats
★ Fruits
★ Vegetables
★ Exclamations
★ Footwear
★ Famous people

SUGGESTIONS FOR ADD-ONS THAT HAVE AN ORDER AND CHANGE

★ Months
★ Numbers in Spanish
★ Presidents
★ Letters of the alphabet
★ Planets

Isolations

Two or more actors

When an actor becomes a character, her entire body changes. For example, if you are playing a sad person, your body might be slouched to show how sad you are; if you are playing a peacock, your body might be proud, and you would move like a bird. When you "isolate" a part of your body, you move only that part. Try to keep the rest of your body as still as possible. **Isolations** warm up your body and help you prepare to become different characters.

One person reads through this exercise while the other players follow the instructions.

Close your eyes and take a deep breath. Relax and let it out slowly. Now you are ready to do isolations.

Isolate your head. Drop your head down so your chin touches your chest. Roll your head slowly to the left so your left ear touches your left shoulder, then to the right. Repeat three times.

Isolate your shoulders. Roll them up to your ears, then back, then down, then front. Reverse the direction so you are rolling them up to your ears, then front, then down, then back. Repeat three times. For a challenge, try rolling one backward and one forward at the same time!

Isolate your arms. Shake them out. With your arms outstretched to the side, make five little circles forward with your arms, then five little circles backward. Make five big circles forward, then five big circles backward.

Isolate your hands. With your arms outstretched in front of you, shake your hands away from you and say, "Good-bye, good-bye, good-bye." Shake them toward you and say, "Come here, come here, come here." Repeat five times, getting faster each time.

Isolate your rib cage, right above your waist where your ribs are. Put your hands on your hips to help with this isolation movement. Move your rib cage from side to side without moving the rest of your body.

Isolate your hips. Make big circles by rotating your hips one way in a circular motion, then the other. Repeat three times. Now make little circles with your hips one way, then the other. Repeat three times.

Isolate your knees. Bend your knees and move your right knee side to side, then your left knee, without moving the top part of your body. Try moving both knees at the same time. Do this three times.

Last but not least, isolate your feet. Shake them out really good, one at a time. Wiggle your toes; then rotate your ankles. Do this three times for each side.

Take another deep breath, and let it out slowly.

 Play It Again, Sam!

To warm up your voice and body at the same time, add a sound effect for each movement.

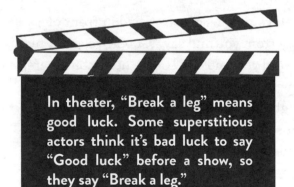

In theater, "Break a leg" means good luck. Some superstitious actors think it's bad luck to say "Good luck" before a show, so they say "Break a leg."

W-o-o-o-h-h-h!

Echo

Two or more actors

This game works best in a theater or large room. The running in this game warms up the body and gives you energy; the speaking helps with projection; and the repeating teaches listening.

If you're in a theater, everyone needs to go to the back of the house (where the audience sits) and line up in the last row. If you're in a room, everyone lines up in the back of the room. The first person in line chooses a sentence. It can be any sentence you like, but it should be easy for everyone to remember, such as, "Jack jumped over the candlestick." The first person in line runs onstage (or to the front of the room), stops center stage, faces the audience, and says the sentence loudly and clearly so everyone else, in the back of the room, can hear "Jack jumped over the candlestick!" If everyone heard and understood the sentence, they repeat it the exact same way. Everyone should also copy the posture and movements of the speaker. If someone cannot hear or understand the first person's sentence, they yell, "What?" and the person tries again. Once this person repeats the sentence, they run to the end of the line while the second person in line runs up onstage or to the front of the room for her turn. The activity continues until everyone has had a turn. Then you can change the sentence and start over.

 Play It Again, Sam!

Play **Name Echo**. For a first rehearsal or a first class, you can use this exercise to learn each other's names by making your sentence "Hello, my name is _____." Then you follow the rest of the rules to **Echo**.

Play **Favorite Line Echo**. If you're working on a play, each player says his favorite line from the play.

Play **Character Echo**. Keep the same sentence but call out different kinds of characters. All players must then say the line the way they think the character might say it, including characteristic body movements and voice changes.

SUGGESTIONS FOR CHARACTER ECHO

- ★ Cheerleader
- ★ Monster
- ★ Teacher
- ★ Opera singer
- ★ Nerd
- ★ Movie star
- ★ Witch
- ★ Old lady

Try **Emotions Echo**. Keep the same sentence but call out different emotions, such as happy, sad, angry, or scared. Players then say the same line but with the selected emotion.

Character of the Space

An actor should always be familiar with the space in which he or she is acting. This activity helps you get to know your space, warm up your body, and practice using your body in different ways.

Walk around the space you're in. It can be a theater, a classroom, a living room, or any open space. Keep walking; only now pretend you're walking through pudding. Think about what it feels like and how your body would move through pudding. For example, you might move more slowly because pudding is thicker than air. After a while, pretend the space has turned into clouds. Think about what that feels like, and how you might walk through clouds.

The space can turn into all sorts of things. Someone is appointed the caller, and whenever she calls out a new type of space, change the way you move.

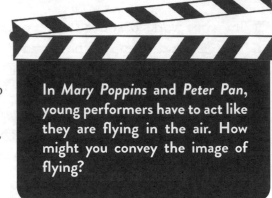

In *Mary Poppins* and *Peter Pan*, young performers have to act like they are flying in the air. How might you convey the image of flying?

PUDDING!

SUGGESTIONS FOR DIFFERENT KINDS OF SPACES

★ Honey
★ Snow
★ Water
★ Mashed potatoes
★ Outer space
★ Popcorn
★ Wind
★ Feathers
★ Mud
★ Fire
★ Taffy
★ Pea soup
★ Tar

Space Walk

Three or more actors

Space Walk is just like **Character of the Space**. It doesn't involve walking in outer space; it means you are exploring the space you are in.

Space walks are a great tool that can be used for hundreds of different theater and creative exercises. Here are two examples of what a leader might say as he or she leads the space walk.

BLOB

"As you are walking around the space, hold an imaginary blob of shapeable material, such as clay or dough. Play with it as you walk. Explore it. See what it can do. How does it smell? How does it taste? What color is it? Make a new discovery about it, something you didn't notice before. Continue to play with it. See what it can do. How heavy is it? What does it feel like in your hands? Make another new discovery about it.

"Now find a partner and combine your two blobs together into one. Play with the new blob together. Explore what it's like now. Imagine how it has changed. Is it bigger? Is it heavier? Make discoveries about it together. Know how it smells now and what color it is."

After about a minute say, "Now find another pair and put your blobs together. Play with it together and see what it can do now. How big has it become? How has it changed? Be playful and explore it together."

Continue the exercise until the entire group has combined into one huge blob. End with all of them working together to throw it out of the room.

EMOTIONS ONE THROUGH TEN

"Walk around the space as if you are happy. See how you walk when you are happy and how your body moves. Imagine that, on a scale of one to ten, you are currently a five of happy. Now bring that up to a six. Heighten the happiness just a bit. Show it in the way you walk around the space. Now bring it up to an eight. Exaggerate the happiness. Show it in your walk and on your face. Now bring it all the way up to a ten. You are the very happiest you can possibly be. Observe how it has changed the way you move.

"Now bring happy back down to a five. You are the average amount of happy. Now go down to a three. You are less happy. Are you walking slower? How has your expression changed? Now go all the way down to a one. You are the complete opposite of happy. How do you walk now? What is your expression like? How do you feel?"

Repeat the exercise with different emotions, including scared and angry.

Silent Disco Dance Party

Five or more actors

Here is a fun twist on space walks. It is a space walk on its head—literally if you'd like. It's a party where anything can happen.

One player is the leader and keeps the rhythm during the game. You can use half of an old cymbal or a hand drum, or you can clap your hands—any beat will do.

The leader says, "Silence! It is time for a silent disco dance party. Everybody dance! It's a party, so go crazy . . . silently."

Then, after a few moments, the leader says, "Stop!" The leader stops the beat, and all the players freeze.

The leader then gives a creative direction, such as, "You're dancing on an iceberg. Go!" All players continue the dance party as if they are on an iceberg. The leader can encourage the dancing by saying things like, "Feel the chill," "Slide down the ice," and "Party with the penguins."

Whenever the leader says, "Stop!" everyone freezes and awaits the new direction. Any direction is fair game. The crazier, the better.

SUGGESTIONS FOR DIRECTIONS

★ Environments, such as on an iceberg, underwater, or the 1920s
★ Conditions, such as, "The room is filled with banana laffy taffy," or "The floor is covered in marbles"
★ Mind-benders, such as, "Tuesdays don't exist," or "Your elbows and your knees have switched."

The silliness of the suggestions is counterbalanced by the seriousness with which they are presented. Remember it's a *silent* disco dance party. Have fun . . . silently!

Play It Again, Sam!

Play **Shoe Character of the Space**. Pretend you have on different kinds of shoes. Whenever a new shoe is called, change the way you move.

SUGGESTIONS FOR DIFFERENT KINDS OF SHOES

- ★ Roller skates
- ★ Space boots
- ★ Moccasins
- ★ Ballet slippers
- ★ Ice skates
- ★ Tap shoes
- ★ Tennis shoes
- ★ Cowboy boots
- ★ Cleats
- ★ Motorcycle boots
- ★ High heels

Play **Color Character of the Space**. Imagine what it would be like if you could walk through colors. Think about what each color means to you and how it makes you feel. Whenever a different color is called, see how it changes the way you move. For example, red might make you feel hot. Move your body to show that you are very hot.

Attention!

This is an "exploring the space" exercise with a playful twist. It also works as an icebreaker or a get-to-know-you game, because you get to share personal information, such as your favorite things.

All players walk around the space until the leader calls, "Attention!" Then all players quickly assemble into a straight line. The leader then asks a question like, "What is your favorite movie?" Starting with the first person in line, everyone quickly answers the question. It's OK if two people choose the same movie. After everyone has said his or her favorite movie, the leader gives the following direction: "Explore the space as if you are in that movie." All the players walk around the space, imagining they are in a scene from their favorite movie. Then the leader calls, "Attention!" and again they line up for a new question and a new direction.

SUGGESTIONS FOR QUESTIONS AND DIRECTIONS

★ What food do you like the least? Explore the space eating that food.

★ What is your favorite animal? Explore the space as that animal.

★ What gift do you wish someone would give you right now? Explore the space imagining someone has just given you that gift.

★ Who is your favorite super hero? Become that hero and explore the space.

★ Where would you like to visit? Explore the space pretending it is that place.

★ What job would you never want to have? Explore the space doing that job.

★ Who is your oldest living relative? Explore the space as that person.

★ What was your last Halloween costume? Explore the space as that character.

★ What makes you happy? Explore the space interacting with that thing.

Little Sally Walker

Two
or more
actors

Here's a give-and-take warm-up game where you create your own dance moves while chanting a fun song.
The words are:

> *Little Sally Walker walking down the street.*
> *She didn't know what to do, so she walked up to me.*
> *I said,*
> *Hey girl, do your dance, do your dance switch.*
> *Hey girl, do your dance, do your dance switch.*

Everyone stands in a circle. One player is chosen to be the first Little Sally Walker. "Sally" stands in the middle of the circle during the first line of the song. Sally approaches another player in the circle and stands directly in front of him for the second line of the song. Sally does her own dance moves for the third line of the song, and the player she is facing mirrors her. On the word "switch," the two players switch places. They do the same dance one more time together on the last line of the song. Then the new player in the middle of the circle becomes the new "Sally" and continues the game.

Show Us How to Get Down!

This is a call-and-response game that lets all the players do their own thing.

Choose one player to stand in the middle, such as Jack. Then recite the following:

PLAYERS:

Hey Jack!

JACK:

Hey what?

PLAYERS:

Hey Jack!

JACK:

Hey what?

PLAYERS:

Show us how to get down!

JACK:

No way.

PLAYERS:

Show us how to get down!

JACK:

OK.

ALL *(as Jack dances in his own way)*:

D-O-W-N, and that's the way to get down!

ALL *(repeating Jack's dance)*:

D-O-W-N, and that's the way to get down!

HEY WHAT?

Great Minds

Two or more actors

It's great for scene partners and groups to be able to think alike. This game is played until two great minds think exactly alike.

Everyone sits in a circle. Two players who are next to each other look at each other, count to three, and say any word at the same time. For example one player says "pizza" at the same time another player says "fireworks."

Next, the person who was on the left turns to the person on his left. They have to try to find a connection between pizza and fireworks. They count to three together and say out loud a word they can think of to connect "pizza" and "fireworks." For example, one may say "America" and the other "carnival." The person on the left of that pair turns to the person on her left in the circle. They now have to try to find a word to connect "America" and "carnival." They

count to three and say their word at the same time, such as "park" and "ride." This game continues until the same word is said at the same time.

Here's an example of how to play: Mike, Diego, Josh, and Rachel are sitting in a circle.

MIKE AND DIEGO:	One, two, three.
MIKE:	Fireworks.
DIEGO:	Pizza.

The words to connect are "fireworks" and "pizza."

DIEGO AND JOSH:	One, two, three.
DIEGO:	America
JOSH:	Carnival.

Now the words to connect are "America" and "carnival."

JOSH AND RACHEL:	One, two, three.
JOSH:	Park.
RACHEL:	Ride.

Now the words to connect are "park" and "ride."

RACHEL AND MIKE:	One, two, three.
RACHEL AND MIKE:	Slide.

The game is over because their two great minds thought alike and both said "slide."

★ 3

Anytime Theater Games

W hether you're an actor or you just want to become more comfortable speaking aloud and thinking on your feet, you will enjoy playing the games in this chapter. They inspire creativity and will spark your imagination. You can play them just about anywhere and teach them to others. Many make great travel games, too.

Listening and working together are important theater skills. Actors need to respond to others' words and movements, and they need to listen to the director. You can practice your listening skills with such games as **Talking Ball**, **One-Word Story**, and **Grocery Store**. Cooperation skills are taught in **One-Word Story** and **Machines**.

Both activities will give you the opportunity to work with other actors as you create.

For ice breakers, try **Blue Ball, Red Ball** and **Silent Scream**. Even the shyest of people have been known to come out of their shells for **The Attention Game**. **Change Three Things** will make you carefully observe and study your partner. The last game in this chapter is **Detective Handshake**. This is a dramatic and mysterious game. It's a favorite at parties and in camp groups.

Open up your mind, and have fun as you play these theater games anytime and anywhere.

In ancient Greece, plays often took place in the marketplace.

Talking Ball

Talking Ball is a creative listening game and involves beginning improvisation. "Improvisation" (also known as "improv") is a drama that is created on the spur of the moment, without any advance preparation; that is, you make it up as you go along. **Talking Ball** is a game that is the basis for more advanced improv games, such as **Conduct a Story** (chapter 5).

PROPS

★   A ball

Sit in a circle (or across from the other person, if two people are playing). One person holds the ball; while he holds the ball, he is the storyteller. The storyteller begins telling a story about anything. After a few sentences, the storyteller tosses the ball to someone else. Now she is the new storyteller. The new storyteller continues the story where the old storyteller left off. The second person must build off of the story that was started by the first person. After a few sentences, the ball is passed again, and the story continues with a new storyteller. Keep tossing the ball until the story comes to an end.

You can only talk if you are holding the talking ball. You can toss the ball at the end of a sentence or in the middle. If the ball is tossed in the middle, the new storyteller continues the story exactly from where the first person stopped. For example, the storyteller may say, "There once was a dog named Rex. He had a friend named . . . ," and tosses the ball. The new storyteller completes the sentence by saying, "Rover," and continues the story.

Listen closely to the story so that, when it's your turn to be the storyteller, everything makes sense.

Here's an example of how this game might work.

> **SALLY** (*holding the talking ball*):
>> Once upon a time, there was a giant who lived on the moon. He was lonely, so he decided to build a spaceship to visit planet earth.

Sally tosses the ball to Henry.

> **HENRY** (*holding the talking ball*):
>> He built his spaceship out of cheese, but he didn't notice all of the mice who were spying on him. That night, when he went to sleep . . .

Henry tosses the ball to Courtney.

COURTNEY *(holding the talking ball)*:

The mice ate holes in his spaceship. They ate so much they couldn't move. They fell asleep in the spaceship.

Courtney tosses the ball to Sally.

SALLY *(holding the talking ball)*:

When the giant woke up, he started up his spaceship. He didn't notice the holes. He landed in Switzerland, which was perfect because his spaceship was made out of Swiss cheese. He and the mice lived happily ever after. The end.

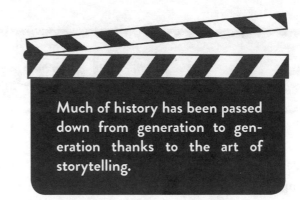

Much of history has been passed down from generation to generation thanks to the art of storytelling.

 Play It Again, Sam!

Going on a long trip? Play **Talking Tap**. Instead of tossing a ball when it's time to pass the story along, tap someone on the shoulder.

One-Word Story

Two
or more
actors

This game is more difficult than **Talking Ball**. **One-Word Story** is the basis for such improv games as **Dr. Know-It-All** (chapter 5). Be ready to listen and think quickly!

Sit in a circle (or across from the other person, if only two people are playing.) Start telling a story, one word at a time, going around the circle (or back and forth with only two players). For example, in a four person game:

AMANDA:	Once—
JONAH:	Upon—
HANNAH:	A—
DANNY:	Time—
AMANDA:	There—
JONAH:	Was—
HANNAH:	A—
DANNY:	Little—
AMANDA:	Cow.

Try not to pause. There are no wrong answers in this game. Just say the first word that pops into your head and see if the story makes sense. It's OK if the person after you doesn't say what you thought he or she would say. It's OK if you're not sure what the person before you is thinking. Continue the story until it comes to an end.

 Play It Again, Sam!

Think of three words that have nothing to do with each other, such as "shoelace," "pickle," and "Ohio." Try to use them in **One-Word Story**.

Play **One-Word-Story Ball**. Instead of telling the story in a circle, toss a ball to someone as you say one word. That person says the next word in a sentence as he or she tosses the ball to someone else, and so on.

Play **One-Word-Story Energy Ball**. Toss an imaginary energy ball to the person who says the next word.

Try **Dr. Know-It-All** (page 73).

Grocery Store

Grocery Store is a warm-up game, because you must run while speaking clearly. It's also a quick-thinking game that involves listening and using your imagination.

PROPS

★ Two chairs

★ A wall with room to run about ten feet in front of it

Set the chairs about ten feet from the wall, with the backs of the chairs to the wall. Pretend the chairs are shopping carts. Each person stands by his or her shopping cart, facing the wall. On the count of three, the first person runs to the wall, grabs a pretend food item, and loudly and clearly calls out the name of the item. Then, as this person runs back to her cart, the second person runs to the wall and grabs another food item. The game continues until someone gets out. But how do you get out?

RULES

1. If you repeat an item that has been said already, you're out.

2. If you pause or take too long to name your item, you're out.

3. If you don't speak loudly and clearly so your partner can hear you, you're out.

4. If you say something that cannot be bought at a grocery store, you're out.

Here's an example of how this game might work.
Jason runs to the wall and pretends to grab an item.

    JASON: Cereal!

Jason runs back to his chair.
Emaline runs to the wall and pretends to grab an item.

    EMALINE: Hot dogs!

Emaline runs back to her chair.
Jason runs to the wall and pretends to grab an item.

    JASON: Spaghetti!

Jason runs back to his chair.
Emaline runs to the wall and pretends to grab an item.

    EMALINE: Cat food!

Emaline runs back to her chair.
Jason runs to the wall and pretends to grab an item.

    JASON: Milk!

Jason runs back to his chair.
Emaline runs to the wall and pretends to grab an item.

    EMALINE: Cereal!

Emaline is out, because cereal has already been said.

Machines

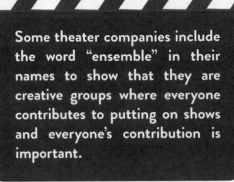

Four or more actors

This is an ensemble-building game. An "ensemble" is a group of people who work together for a common purpose. In this case, the purpose is to make a machine. This game will also help you overcome any fear you may have about feeling or looking silly. Just let loose and really become the machine.

First, decide what kind of machine you want to make. It can be a real machine, such as a washing machine or a blender, or you can make up a new kind of machine, such as a monster machine or peace machine. One person starts by making a sound and coming up with a movement that is part of the machine. (Try to choose a movement that involves your entire body. Think about what kind of sounds the machine might make.) The first person repeats her sound and movement over and over, as if the machine were running. While she is doing this, the next person connects to her and creates his own movement and sound. To connect, you don't actually have to touch the other person, but make sure it is clear that you are part of the same machine. Once all the actors are connected to the machine, the machine begins to speed up. It gets faster and faster until it's going so fast that it breaks down, and all parts of the machine collapse. Everyone falls to the floor, and the machine comes to an end.

The object of this game is to work together to make sure the machine gets faster and faster, at the same pace, and breaks down all at once. Be sure to keep your own sound and movement throughout the entire machine. Even though you are listening to and working with others, keep doing your own thing.

Some theater companies include the word "ensemble" in their names to show that they are creative groups where everyone contributes to putting on shows and everyone's contribution is important.

SUGGESTIONS FOR KINDS OF MACHINES

★ Pizza machine
★ Telephone
★ Laughing machine
★ Computer
★ Taffy-making machine
★ Snowblower
★ The human body
★ Can opener
★ Pollution machine
★ Music machine

Blue Ball, Red Ball

Six or more actors

This warm-up game demonstrates many useful skills, including teamwork, give-and-take, and listening.

Players stand in a circle. A leader tosses an imaginary ball to someone and tells him or her that it is the blue ball. That player catches the imaginary blue ball and says, "Thank you, blue ball," to the leader, then turns to another player and tosses the ball to him, saying, "Blue ball." The blue ball continues to be passed from player to player. Meanwhile, the leader starts a red ball.

The object of the game is to keep each imaginary ball going as the color it started. See how many different balls you can keep going in your group. Be sure to always tell the person you are tossing it to what color it is and to always thank the person who gave it to you, repeating its color so that person knows you received it correctly.

 ## Play It Again, Sam!

Play **Emotion Ball**. Instead of playing with balls of different colors, name the balls for emotions, such as happy ball, sad ball, and angry ball. Take on the ball's emotion when you are holding it.

Play it as a **Space Walk**. Instead of standing in a circle, walk around the space you are in and have players hand the different balls to people as they walk by.

Silent Scream

How many different kinds of screams are there? Play this game to see how well you can communicate to the audience what's going on when someone screams.

Divide into two groups. Sit or stand facing each other so that everyone can see the other team. If the group is large, have some folks sit in front while others stand behind them.

Team A gives team B something to scream about. It could be a good thing, a bad thing, a scary thing, an exciting thing, or anything else you can think of. On the count of three, team B poses like they are screaming about the given subject. They don't make any sound. They show on their face and in their bodies what it's like to scream like that. Team B should continue to hold the freeze while team A says some observations. What can they tell about the way team B is posing? How do they feel?

After a few observations have been made, team B takes their turn in giving team A something to scream about. Continue the game until each team has tried a variety of screams.

SUGGESTIONS FOR SCREAMS

★ A scary movie
★ A surprise party
★ Spoiled milk
★ A roller coaster
★ A stubbed toe
★ An annoying sibling
★ A spider
★ Just finding out you're going to be in a movie
★ A rock concert
★ Seeing a car crash
★ Parachuting

The Attention Game

Four actors

Even the shyest of people open up for this game. This game is so competitive you might not notice how well you're improvising!

PROPS

★ Three chairs
★ A stopwatch or a watch with a second hand

Place the three chairs in a row with an actor sitting on each chair. The fourth person stands close by and keeps track of the time. The person in the middle chair is the listener. She has a very important job. The two actors sitting on either side of the listener compete for her attention by talking about interesting things or making funny noises.

On the count of three, the actors on the outside chairs have thirty seconds to talk to the listener at the same time. The goal is to attract the listener's attention. At the end of thirty seconds, the listener decides which of the two actors captured more of her attention.

RULES

1. The talkers must stay in their chairs.
2. The talkers cannot touch the listener.

 Play It Again, Sam!

Play this game in front of an audience. Take topic suggestions from the audience and use these to try and attract the listener's attention. For example, the person on the listener's right might talk about sports, while the person on the listener's left talks about food. Let the audience help the listener judge who attracts the most attention.

Change Three Things

An even number of actors

This is an observation and memorization game. If you concentrate, you will do very well at this game.

The group splits in half. Now there are two groups. Each group forms a line and faces the other group. Your partner is the person standing directly across from you. Everyone plays this game at the same time. Spend a few minutes looking over your partner. Notice every detail from the top of his head to the tip of his toes—how he styles his hair, whether he's wearing a vest, if his shoes are tied, if his socks are up or down, and so on.

After a few minutes, all players turn around so that they are facing away from their partners. Each player changes three things about themselves. It can be something as obvious as tucking in your shirt or as subtle as putting a ring on another finger.

After everyone has changed three things, everyone turns around and faces his or her partner again. Take a few minutes to look over your partner and try to figure out what three things have changed about him or her. Go down the line and see if everyone can guess what three things are different about his or her partner.

Detective Handshake

Six or more actors

Everyone likes a good mystery. This game lets you be the detective, the victim, and sometimes even the killer! You can practice being very dramatic with this game. Also your powers of observation are very important here—just like a good detective.

One player is selected to start. Everyone else sits down and closes his or her eyes. The selected player walks around the room and pats one person on the head. This person will be the killer. After the selected player has chosen a killer, she says, "Welcome to my _____ party." She fills in the blank with her favorite kind of party—tea party, slumber party, or birthday party.

Next, all the players get up and act as if they are at that kind of a party. Everyone walks around the room and shakes hands with the other party guests. If the killer wants to kill someone, she gently scratches the inside of her victim's hand when she shakes it. The victim then waits ten seconds before dying a great, dramatic death. Then that person is out of the game. (It's very important to wait ten seconds—and even shake other peoples' hands during that time—so you don't give away who the killer is.)

When someone thinks he knows who the killer is, he makes a guess. But if he guesses wrong, he must die a great, dramatic death, too! The game continues until someone who has not been killed correctly guesses who the killer is.

If you want to play again, the player who correctly guesses who the killer is gets to choose the next killer and a new kind of party.

RULES

1. A guess cannot be made until at least one person has been killed.

2. The killer does not have to kill everyone whose hand he or she shakes.

3. You cannot refuse to shake someone's hand. If you think he or she is the killer, make a guess.

Don't forget to behave like you are at a particular kind of party. For example, if it's a tea party, pretend to be drinking tea as you shake hands; for a slumber party, you can be setting up your sleeping bag; for a birthday party, you might be eating cake. Also be sure to die a great, dramatic death, complete with sound effects.

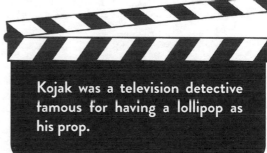

Kojak was a television detective famous for having a lollipop as his prop.

Theater in the Round

(Games Played in a Circle)

The games in this chapter are for groups to play standing or sitting in a circle. They make good party games or can be used as actor warm-ups.

Want to Buy a . . . is a memorization game. It can help you memorize your lines for a play, rehearse for an oral report, or memorize facts for a test.

People of all ages sometimes have trouble focusing their attention. **Zoom**, **Thumper**, **Guess the Leader**, **Pass the Clap**, and **Zip Zap Zop** are all excellent focusing activities.

Important basic acting and improv concepts (see chapter 7) are taught in **Give-and-Take** and **Yes And**.

Listening skills are further developed in **This Is a . . .** and **Operator**, which is a favorite at indoor parties. These games require no setup.

Knots promotes team building and skills for working in groups—skills valuable in theater as well as everyday life.

Just like the gears of a watch or the parts of a machine, circles are for working together. Everyone is connected and cooperating with everyone else.

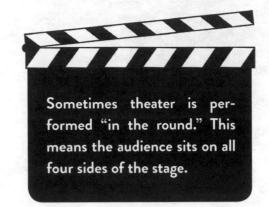

Sometimes theater is performed "in the round." This means the audience sits on all four sides of the stage.

Want to Buy a . . .

Four or more actors

Memorizing lines is an important part of an actor's job. This is a memorization and listening game that can get really crazy.

Sit in a circle. If you are chosen to start the game, turn to the player on your left and say, "Do you want to buy a . . . ?" Fill in the blank with any object or animal that you think of—for example, a pig. The person next to you responds by asking, "A what?" and you repeat the animal name: "A pig."

Then the person asks an "Is it" or "Does it" question about the pig, such as, "Does it oink?" You answer the question with, "Of course it oinks."

This second person then turns to the third person in the circle and says, "Do you want to buy a . . . ?" He or she fills in the blank with a new animal or object, such as a car. The third person asks, "A what?" and the second person repeats, "A what?" You answer, "A pig," and the second person says, "A car." The third person then asks an "Is it" or "Does it" question about the car, such as, "Is it new?" The second person repeats his or her question about the pig, "Does it oink?" You say, "Of course it oinks." The second person answers the question posed to them with, "Of course it's new."

Now it's the third person's turn to ask the fourth person, "Do you want to buy a . . . ?" and so on. Sound confusing? Just wait until you play it!

Here's an example of how this game might work.

ZACK:
Do you want to buy a dog?

ANNA *(to Zack)*:
A what?

ZACK *(to Anna)*:
A dog.

ANNA *(to Zack)*:
Does it bark?

ZACK *(to Anna)*:
Of course it barks.

ANNA *(to Joshua, on her left)*:
Do you want to buy an apple?

JOSHUA *(to Anna)*:
A what?

ANNA *(to Zack)*:
A what?

ZACK *(to Anna)*:
A dog.

ANNA *(to Joshua)*:

    An apple.

JOSHUA *(to Anna)*:

    Is it red?

ANNA *(to Zack)*:

    Does it bark?

ZACK *(to Anna)*:

    Of course it barks.

ANNA *(to Joshua)*:

    Of course it's red.

JOSHUA *(to Becky)*:

    Do you want to buy a fish?

BECKY *(to Joshua)*:

    A what?

To memorize his lines, an actor may tape record the other character's lines, leaving space on the tape for his lines. Then, he can play the tape back and say his lines when the right time comes.

JOSHUA *(to Anna)*:

    A what?

ANNA *(to Zack)*:

    A what?

ZACK *(to Anna)*:

    A dog.

ANNA *(to Joshua)*:

    An apple.

JOSHUA *(to Becky)*:

    A fish.

BECKY *(to Joshua)*:

    Does it swim?

JOSHUA *(to Anna)*:

    Is it red?

ANNA *(to Zack)*:

    Does it bark?

ZACK *(to Anna)*:

    Of course it barks.

ANNA *(to Joshua)*:

    Of course it's red.

JOSHUA *(to Becky)*:

    Of course it swims.

Whew!

Zoom

Four or more actors

Think of the sound a car makes as it's zooming by: "Zoom!" Now think of the sound a car makes when it screeches to a sudden stop: "Errrrr!" This activity lets you use your imagination, gets you focused, and helps you practice sound effects.

Sit in a circle and wind up an imaginary car. Make a winding-up sound with your voice as you do this. Set the imaginary car on the floor in front of you, push it with your hand to the person next to you, and say, "Zoom!" That person pushes it along to the next person, saying, "Zoom!" The car continues around the circle, "Zoom!" "Zoom!" "Zoom!" This continues until someone stops it by putting out his or her hand and making the loud screeching sound: "Errrrr!" That person changes the direction of the car, and pushes it the other way, saying, "Zoom!"

When the car comes to you, you have two choices:

1. Push it in the same direction it is already going, saying, "Zoom!" or

2. Stop it by putting out your hand, saying "Errrrr!" then pushing it back the way it came, saying, "Zoom!"

The only way to change the direction of the car is to stop it first. If the car gets lost (if you don't know who has it or where it was last), start over by winding it up again.

Here are more elements you can add to make **Zoom** even more fun and challenging.

1. Pit Stop: Place both hands out in front of you and say, "Pit stop." This makes the car skip the next person in the circle.

2. Oil Slick: Make a circle in the air with your finger as you say, "Oil slick." This causes the car to change direction *and* skip the next person in the circle.

3. Ramp: Lift your arms up diagonally toward the next person. That person screams, and the next person lifts his arms up to become the other half of the bridge. The player next to him continues with the game.

4. Suspension Bridge: Same as Ramp, except two players scream instead of one.

5. Traffic: Point to someone across the circle and say, "Traffic." You then switch places with that person nice and slowly while the other players yell at you as if you are holding up traffic. After you both rejoin the circle, the person you pointed to continues with the game.

6. Gattica: When you say, "Gattica," you start the zoom going in both directions at the same time. When they both come back to you after going all the way around the circle, you continue the game in the regular way.

7. Hyperspace: Push an imaginary button in front of you and say, "Hyperspace." Then another player somewhere else in the circle starts with a zoom. It doesn't matter who the player is—it's just whoever is the first player to do it.

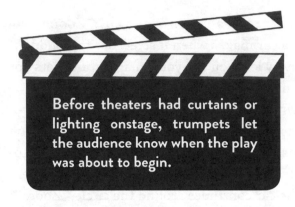

Before theaters had curtains or lighting onstage, trumpets let the audience know when the play was about to begin.

Guess the Leader

Six or more actors

To be successful at this game, you must focus, pay close attention, and observe everyone around you. Because this game requires no equipment and little explanation, it's a great transition game when you have extra time you didn't know you'd have.

Sit in a circle. Choose one person to leave the room while the remaining players choose another person to be the leader. The leader starts a movement, such as patting her knees. The other players follow by mirroring her movement. The leader changes the movement periodically, and everyone else in the group mirrors her action. The outside player, or guesser, comes back into the room and stands in the middle of the circle. The guesser has three chances to guess who the leader is.

The leader can choose any movement that the other players can do, too. For example, the leader can clap her hands for a while, then change to patting her head. Everyone continues to mirror the leader until the guesser correctly identifies the leader or has used up his or her three guesses.

For the next round, the leader leaves the room to become the guesser, and a new leader is chosen. Continue playing until everyone has a chance to lead and to guess.

Acting tip for the leader: Don't make any sudden changes in movement. Let the movements flow from one into the next so that everyone else can easily follow this change.

Acting tip for the guesser: Use your ears as well as your eyes. For example, when the movement changes to a clap, see if you can tell where the sound of the clap first came from.

Acting tip for the other players: Don't look right at the leader. If everyone is looking at the leader, it's very easy for the guesser to identify her.

Pass the Clap

You can learn the basic concept of "give-and-take" with this activity while practicing rhythm, too!

Stand in a circle. Turn to the person on your left, make eye contact with him, and clap together. The goal is to clap at the same time. Next, he turns to the person on his left, makes eye contact, and claps at the same time as that person. Keep passing the clap around the circle. See if you can pass it in rhythm.

Be sure to focus and make eye contact as you take and give the clap. Always be ready for it, and keep it going smoothly around the circle. See how fast you can go.

 Play It Again, Sam!

Sing a song as you pass the clap. Keep the clap going with the rhythm of the song. "Take Me Out to the Ball Game" is a great song for this activity. Try slow songs and fast songs. Just remember to focus and keep the rhythm.

Zip Zap Zop

Four or more actors

This is probably one of the most famous theater warm-up games. **Zip Zap Zop** combines quick thinking with fast movements.

Before you play, practice jumping, clapping, and pointing at the same time. OK, since you can't actually clap and point at the exact same time, practice jumping and clapping and then pointing right after you clap.

The second thing you need to remember is the title of the game, in the right order: zip, zap, zop.

Stand in a circle. One person starts by jumping, clapping, and pointing to someone as she says, "Zip." The person she points to jumps, claps, and points to someone else, saying, "Zap." The person she points to then jumps, claps, and points to someone else, saying, "Zop." The person he points to then jumps, claps, and points to someone else, saying, "Zip." The game continues until someone gets out.

RULES

1. If you don't say the right word, you're out. Remember, it's always "zip, zap, zop." Then it starts all over again with "zip."

2. If it's not clear who you pointed to, you're out, so be sure to point directly at someone and make eye contact with her.

3. If you pause or wait too long when it's your turn, you're out. When you're out, have a seat and help judge when others get out by breaking one or more of the rules. Continue playing until one person is left.

 Play It Again, Sam!

Play **Tongue Twister Zip Zap Zop**. Instead of saying "zip," "zap," and "zop," say the words to your favorite tongue twister or song. "Peter Piper" works great. Just jump, clap, and point to someone saying, "Peter." The person you pointed to jumps, claps, and points saying, "Piper." The person he pointed to then jumps, claps, and points, saying, "Picked," and so on.

Give-and-Take

Four or more actors

Give-and-take is an important concept in acting. A good actor knows when to give focus to another actor and when to take focus. If an actor is saying a line, all eyes and ears should be on her. When it is time to say your line, be strong and say it like you mean it in order to take focus.

This game will help you learn the concept of give-and-take. It also helps you lose your inhibitions and not be afraid to get a little crazy.

Stand in a circle. One person is chosen to go into the middle of the circle and make a unique sound and movement. Repeating this sound and movement over and over, he goes up to someone else in the circle and "gives" the person this sound and movement. To "take" a sound and movement, the new person mirrors the giver's actions until she is doing it exactly the same way. When the giver is satisfied that the new person has imitated this sound and movement correctly, he will nod his head.

The new person continues doing the sound and movement while moving into the middle of the circle. The giver takes this second player's place in the circle. The new person makes the sound and movement her own by slowly changing it into a new sound and a new movement. Then she gives the new sound and movement to someone else in the circle, following the same pattern just described.

Continue giving and taking sounds until everyone has had at least one turn. As you get better at this game, you can make your sounds and movements more complicated.

The title song from the musical *Oklahoma* is the official state song of Oklahoma.

Thumper

Thumper combines the focus of **The Number Game** (chapter 2) and the creativity of **Give-and-Take** for a fast-paced, competitive game. This is a great warm-up or energy-boosting activity for your theater group.

Sit in a circle. Pick someone to begin. He picks a short sound and movement that can be done from a seated position, and he performs this sound and movement. Then the person sitting next to him comes up with a different sound and movement and demonstrates it. Continue until everyone has come up with and demonstrated his or her unique sound and movement.

To start the game, choose one person to be the leader. Together, all of the players quickly pat or thump the floor with their hands while saying the following chant:

LEADER:

What's the name of the game?

OTHER PLAYERS:

Thumper!

LEADER:

How do you play?

OTHER PLAYERS:

Fast and easy!

The leader makes her sound and movement and immediately follows this with any other player's sound and movement. This second player makes his sound and movement, then someone else's. (Always make your own first, then somebody else's.) As soon as somebody else makes your sound and movement, it's your turn. When it's not your turn, keep thumping on the floor. The game moves quickly and continues until someone is out.

WHAT'S THE NAME OF THE GAME?

RULES

1. If you pause or wait too long when it's your turn, you're out.

2. If you don't make your own sound and movement first and then follow it with somebody else's, you're out.

3. If you don't get the sound and movement right—for example, you do one person's sound but another person's movement—you're out.

4. If you use someone's sound and movement who is already out, you're out.

When someone gets out, he or she stays in the circle and continues to thump, but that's all.

Start each new round by repeating the chant. The game continues until only one person is left.

 ## Play It Again, Sam!

Play **Animal Thumper**. Everyone's sound and movement must be inspired by an animal. Here are some examples:

★ Flapping your arms like a chicken and saying, "Bok bok"
★ Moving your hands like a snake and saying, "Sssssss"
★ Holding your hands up like you're begging and saying, "Arf arf"
★ Making your arms into an elephant's trunk and sounding like a trumpet
★ Holding your hands up like claws and growling

A real dog performed in the first production of Shakespeare's play *Two Gentlemen of Verona*.

Yes And

Four or more actors

Supporting and cooperating with your fellow actors is an important skill and the basis for acting and improvisation (see chapter 7). To support your partner, agree with her ideas. Say yes to them. To cooperate with your partner, build onto her ideas. This game shows you how to do these things.

Sit in a circle. Make eye contact with someone and say a statement such as, "The grass is green." The player you made eye contact with then makes eye contact with someone else and says, "Yes." Then he repeats your statement, "The grass is green," and adds "and" as well as his own statement, such as, "The sky is blue." The person he made eye contact with then turns to someone else and says, "Yes, the sky is blue, and clowns are funny." Each player repeats the phrase the previous player passed to her and adds her own. The game continues until everyone but one player is out.

How do you get out? Here are the rules.

RULES

1. Always say "yes," then repeat the other player's statement. Follow that with "and"; then add your own statement. If you say "no" or "but," you're out.

2. No pronouns allowed. If you use a pronoun, you're out. Pronouns are words like "she," "he," "it," "I," or "they." Instead of saying, "I like cake," use a name and say, "Lisa likes cake."

3. Be sure to make clear eye contact. If no one can tell who you're looking at, you're out.

4. No pausing. If you take too long to repeat the statement or to say your own statement, you're out.

When you're out, leave the circle and help judge when others get out. Continue playing until one person is left.

THE GRASS IS GREEN

YES AND

This Is a . . .

Four or more actors

Discover working together in rhythm with this game. **This Is a . . .** becomes an intense listening game, because you must hear what is being passed to you at the same time that you must tell the next person what you are passing to them. In addition, everyone is talking at once.

PROPS

★ A different small object for each player (a pencil, key, watch, or rubber band)

Sit in a circle and hold your object in your hand. To begin the activity, every player turns to the player on their left and says, "This is a . . ." You then say the name of whatever object you're holding. Then turn to the person on your right and say, "A what?" Turn back to the person on your left and say, "A . . . ," and the name of the object. Then turn right and say, "A what?" Turn left and say, "A . . . ," and the name of the object. Turn right, take the new object and say, "Oh, a . . . !" Here you fill in the blank with your new object. Continue passing the objects around the circle until you get your original object back.

 ## Play It Again, Sam!

For a challenge, lie about what the object is. Pass a pencil around, but say it's an elephant. See if it comes back to you as an elephant. If you can't understand the person on your right, either say what you thought you heard or call the new object a "something" as you pass it on.

Acting tip: You are responsible for making sure the person on your left hears and understands you. That is your job. Don't worry about hearing the person on your right. They are responsible for you. If everyone takes care of the person on his or her left, the game will be successful. Just like in theater, if you take care of your scene partners, you won't have to be nervous because they'll take care of you.

Operator

Four or more actors

This is a quiet listening game that requires no preparation. The object of this game is to pass a message all the way around the circle so that it ends up being the same message as when it began.

Sit in a circle, and begin the game with one player whispering a sentence or phrase to the player on his right. That person whispers the same message to the person on her right, and this continues until it gets all the way around to the person on your left. The person on your left says the message out loud. You then repeat the original message out loud. If the message is the same, then you succeeded! If the message is not the same, it's funny to hear how it changed.

RULES

1. If, for example, Megan doesn't hear the message, she can say, "Operator," and the player sending the message must repeat it.

2. You may only say operator once. After that, you have to pass the message along as best you can, even if it's not quite right.

Here's an example of how this game might work.

SOPHIE *(whispering to Noah)*:
> The big green frog ate ten flies for lunch.

NOAH *(whispering to Megan)*:
> The big green frog ate ten flies for lunch.

MEGAN *(not hearing what Noah says)*:
> Operator!

NOAH *(repeating the message, whispering again to Megan)*:
> The big green frog ate ten flies for lunch.

MEGAN *(still doesn't hear it quite right but cannot say operator again, so she whispers to Todd what she thinks she heard)*:
> A big dog ate a bunch of fleas at ten o'clock.

TODD *(the last in the circle, says out loud)*:
> The big dog ate a bunch of fleas at ten o'clock.

SOPHIE:
> That's not what I said. I said, "The big green frog ate ten flies for lunch!"

Well, they were close.

Knots

his is a game for people who want to learn to work together on a play, team, school project, or anyplace where you're working closely with others.

Stand in a circle, reach your hands out in front of you, cross them at the elbows, and close your eyes. Everyone slowly steps into the circle and takes hold of the first two hands he or she comes across. Once everyone has found two hands to hold, open your eyes. All of your hands should be knotted up. The goal is to unknot your hands, without letting go, until you're back in a circle. You might have to step over somebody, let someone crawl under you, or twist in crazy ways. Work together to do whatever it takes to get back in a circle.

Five or more actors

 Play It Again, Sam!

Try doing this without speaking. With larger groups, have a **Knot Race**. See which team can straighten out its knot first.

Alien Life Span

Four or more actors

Imagine what the life of an alien might be like. Does it go from baby to old age like humans? Work together to create the life span of an alien.

Players stand in a circle. One player goes in the middle of the circle and is born (or hatches) and shows everyone what the newborn alien is like. Be sure to make the sounds that the newborn alien would make. After a moment, that player crawls to another player. The new player mirrors the newborn alien, then switches places with the first player. The new player crawls to the middle of the circle and portrays the alien when it is a bit older. The new player shows everyone what a toddler alien might act like and sound like. When the toddler alien is established, that player approaches a third player in the circle. The third player mirrors the second player as the toddler alien, then switches places with her. The third player goes into the middle of the circle and makes the alien age a bit more. Now the alien is a child. Continue the game until the alien expires of old age.

Bunny Bunny

Six or more actors

Players stand in a circle. All players begin by patting their hands on their knees in a slow rhythm, saying, "Tonga, tonga, tonga," in low voices.

One person holds her hands as if they are puppets. She turns them in toward her own face and says, "Bunny, bunny," in a medium voice while opening and closing her hands. Then she points her hands at another player and says, "Bunny, bunny," to that person. It is then that player's turn to say, "Bunny, bunny," to himself, then to another player. This is how the turn passes. "Bunny, bunny, bunny, bunny," should be said exactly twice as fast as "Tonga, tonga, tonga."

Whenever anyone is saying "Bunny, bunny," the two players on either side of her face that player, wave their hands in the air, and say, "Toki toki toki toki toki toki toki toki," in a high voice. The speed at which you repeat "toki" should be said exactly twice as fast as the speed at which you repeat "bunny."

Rhythmically, think of "tonga" as a whole note, "bunny" as a half note, and "toki" as a quarter note.

In My Nose

Two or more actors

This is a rhyming rhythm game with a funny tag line. Players sit in a circle. All players should be ready to say the line, "In my nose." This phrase is said between all other lines. Start keeping a rhythm by snapping or patting your legs. The first player starts with a line that is easy to rhyme with, such as, "There's a goat." Then all players say, "In my nose." The player to the right of who started then says a short line that rhymes with goat, such as, "Ride a boat." Then all players say, "In my nose."

See how far around the circle you can get using the same rhyme. Also, try to stay in rhythm.

SUGGESTIONS FOR STARTING LINES THAT ARE EASY TO RHYME WITH

★ There's a cat.
★ I have to blow.
★ There's a stick.
★ I have a cold.
★ Pour some juice.
★ Have a snack.
★ Can you see?

Mr. Hit

Six or more actors

This game is easy to explain but hard to play. It takes a lot of concentration to play this game without messing up.

Players sit in a circle. A leader tells everyone the only two rules of the game:

1. If you hear your name, touch someone next to you.

2. If you get touched, say someone's name.

Sounds easy, but it's hard to do. It is a great way to practice focus.

Here's an example of how to play. Charlie, Ann, Henry, Emma, and Delaney are sitting in a circle.

CHARLIE: Delaney.

Delaney touches Emma.

EMMA: Ann.

Ann touches Henry.

HENRY: Emma.

Emma touches Delaney.

DELANEY: Charlie.

 ## Play It Again, Sam!

To make this game even more difficult, choose an ice-cream flavor or a color for everyone to be and say that instead of names.

Sevens

Three or more actors

This warm-up game makes you think in three different ways at once. You have to listen to the other players, think of items in a category, and count in your head all at the same time.

Players sit in a circle. The first player says a category, such as color. Going around in clockwise order, each of the next seven players says a color. Without pausing to count, the eighth player says another category. The round continues until someone gets out.

Here are the ways you get out:

★ If you repeat an item in a given category, you're out.

★ If you don't say a new category when it's your turn to do so, you're out.

★ If you pause to long, you're out.

This game can be played in small or large groups. In small groups, the players will have to say more than one thing in a given category. The game just continues until seven things have been said.

Suggestion: Rather than players getting "out," try one of these consequences.

1. Assign a "Big Louie" chair. The goal is to sit in this chair, and when someone gets out, they have to go to the chair furthest away from the Big Louie chair. Other players move up when this happens.

2. Play goose-pot-style. The middle of the circle is the "goose pot"; when you are out, you sit in the middle until another player gets out. Then you rejoin the circle.

3. Play H-O-R-S-E-style. Choose a word such as "out." Each time a player messes up, he or she gets a letter. When a player has spelled out the word "out," the game is over.

Here is an example of how to play: Carl, Dexter, Emily, Grace, and Timmy are sitting in a circle. Carl says the first category, and the game continues clockwise:

CARL:
> States.

DEXTER:
> Illinois.

EMILY:
> California.

GRACE:
> Hawaii.

TIMMY:
> Ohio.

CARL:
> Florida.

DEXTER:
> Nevada.

EMILY:
> Alaska.

GRACE:
> Girl names.

Instead of saying another state, Grace changed the category because she is eighth.

TIMMY:
> Hannah.

CARL:
> Michaela.

DEXTER:
> Margo.

EMILY:
> Anna.

GRACE:
> Nancy.

TIMMY:
> Sports teams.

Timmy is out, because he was supposed to say another girl's name instead of a new category.

★ 5

Make 'Em Laugh
(Ideas for Funny Scenes)

....

Theater games can lead to ideas for a creative performance. In fact, theater games have been used by professional theater companies and improv troupes all over the world. The activities in this chapter (as well as the ones in chapter 7, "Improvisation") will give you some ideas for creating comedy scenes. You can combine them to create a comedy variety show or comedy revue that your audience is sure to enjoy.

Conduct a Story brings a storytelling concert to your audience. You can let your audience participate in **Dr. Know-It-All** and **Gripes**. You can play guessing games with your audience in **Three-Word Skits** and **Syllables**. **Act a Joke** and **Commercials** are creative ways to develop original scenes for your performance.

Performing for others is exciting and fun. If you don't have a theater, you can perform in your home or classroom. And even one person can be a good audience—especially when you make 'em laugh.

One of the most famous stage mothers (a parent who dedicates her life to taking her child or children to rehearsals and sitting through them) was Minnie Palmer, the mother of the Marx Brothers. She went to their rehearsals and laughed at all their jokes. The musical *Minnie's Boys* is based on her story.

Conduct a Story

Three or more actors

After you have played **Talking Ball** (chapter 3), try this game to create a concert of creative stories.

One person is the conductor. The other players gather together so they can see the conductor; some stand in back, and some sit in front. Just like at a symphony, begin by tuning and warming up, but instead of using instruments, use your voices. When the conductor gives a signal, such as lifting her arms, everyone warms up by speaking at the same time. Players can talk about anything they like, or they just make sounds with their voices. The conductor cuts them off with another signal, perhaps quickly bringing her arms down. Now you're ready to start the game.

The conductor points to one player, and he begins telling a story. At any time, the conductor can signal to cut him off and have a new person continue by pointing to her. Each new player must continue the story exactly where the last person ended, even if he ended in the middle of a sentence or in the middle of a word. Try to make the story flow as smoothly as possible so that it sounds like one person is telling it.

Here's an example of how this game might work. The conductor gives the signal for the musicians to warm up. All musicians warm up by talking and making noises. The conductor gives the signal to stop warming up. The conductor starts the concert by pointing to Jill.

JILL:

> Once upon a time, a little boy was playing in his yard. Suddenly he noticed—

The conductor stops pointing to Jill and points to Tess.

TESS:

> That a flying saucer was hovering over head. He watched as giant orange beetles flew out of the saucer and landed—

The conductor stops pointing to Tess and points to Marco.

MARCO:

> In the little boy's sandbox. The alien beetles started playing with the sand, when the little boy said, "Excuse me, but this is my sandbox." The aliens said, "If you let us play, we'll teach you how to make a giant dino—

The conductor stops pointing to Marco and points to Tess.

TESS:

> —saur. So they all built a dinosaur out of sand and called it Sammy. The aliens went home, and the little boy got to keep Sammy for a pet. The end.

Notice how, in the last line, Tess had to finish the word "dinosaur," the word that Marco had started.

Dr. Know-It-All

Four
or more
actors

After you have played **One-Word Story** (chapter 3), try this game. Classmates, friends, and parents will especially enjoy the audience participation and the chance to meet a person who knows everything.

PROPS

★ Three chairs
★ A toilet-paper roll or another tubular object that can be used as a microphone

Choose one person to be the announcer. The other three players sit next to each other, in the chairs, facing the audience. The announcer introduces the three as Dr. Know-It-All. The announcement might go something like this:

ANNOUNCER:

> I am proud to present to you the world-famous, brilliant Dr. Know-It-All! Dr. Know-It-All knows it all! Dr. Know-It-All has the answers to all your questions. Let me demonstrate how brilliant he is. Dr. Know-It-All, what is two plus two?

The three seated players who are Dr. Know-It-All answer the question one word at a time, each person in order, just like in the game **One-Word Story**.

ANIKA:

> Two.

GARRETT:

> Plus.

JEAN:

> Two.

ANIKA:

> Equals.

GARRETT:

> Four.

The announcer then invites questions from the audience.

ANNOUNCER:

> Thank you, Dr. Know-It-All! Now are there any questions from the audience?

The announcer calls on someone from the audience who asks a question. The announcer repeats the question, and then Dr. Know-It-All answers it.

RULES

1. It's OK if you don't really know the answer to a question—just make it up. There are no wrong answers in this game.

2. Keep in mind that the three of you are playing one person. So, for example, sit the exact same way. If one part of Dr. Know-It-All changes the way he's sitting, the other two parts must change. Act the same way and take on the same attitude. If one of you acts like the question is silly, all of you must act that way. Try to make the answers flow so smoothly that it sounds like one person is talking.

3. Begin the answer by repeating the question. For example, if the question is, "Why is the sky blue?" Dr. Know-It- All should start the answer with, "The sky is blue because . . ."

Gripes

This is an improv game that gives you a chance to let off some steam. In this game, the conductor makes music by combining different voices and gripes—which is another word for "complaints"—into a symphony of noise.

Just like in **Conduct a Story**, the conductor stands in front of the other players, who gather around so they can see the conductor. The conductor gives everyone a topic to gripe or complain about. (If you're playing this game for a performance, you may take suggestions from the audience.)

After everyone has a gripe, the conductor begins by warming everyone up. The conductor lifts his arms, and all the players warm up their voices by making sounds and noises. When the conductor lowers his arms, everyone stops. Now you're ready to begin the game.

The conductor begins by pointing to a player. She then begins to talk about her assigned gripe. When the conductor cuts her off, she stops griping. But when the conductor points to her again, she continues what she was saying, starting exactly where she left off, even if she was in the middle of a word.

RULES

1. The conductor can point to one player at a time or many players at once.

2. The conductor can signal for the players to get louder or softer.

3. The conductor can signal for one player to get louder while others get softer.

4. The conductor decides when to end the symphony.

SUGGESTIONS FOR GRIPE TOPICS

★ Cafeteria food
★ Cleaning
★ Homework
★ Siblings
★ Bad weather
★ Broken toys
★ Rude people
★ Standing in line

Three-Word Skits

Four or more actors

This is a guessing game that is perfect for groups who enjoy performing for each other. This game can also spark your creative-writing instincts or help you develop a playwriting idea.

Divide into groups (or pairs). Each group must come up with three words that have nothing to do with each other, such as "frog," "telephone," and "basketball." Next, each group quickly makes up and rehearses a scene that uses all three words, but they cannot say these specific words in their scene.

When all the groups are ready, take turns performing scenes for each other. See who can guess your group's three words first.

SUGGESTIONS FOR CREATING GOOD SCENES

★ Interesting scenes have a beginning, middle, and end.
★ Good scenes feature interesting characters.
★ Plan the basics of your scene and rehearse it, but allow room for improvisation, too.

Part of the magic of improv comes from the surprises you can create in the moment.

Syllables

Three or more actors

After you have played **Three-Word Skits**, try this guessing game. While usually played in groups or in front of an audience, this game can be played with as few as two players and one guesser.

With your group or partner, think of a three-syllable word, such as "tornado." Divide your word into syllables like this: "tor-na-do." Your challenge is to figure out how to act out each syllable. For example, for "tor," you can act out the word "tore"; for "na," you can act out the sound horses make; and for "do," act out the word "dough."

Next, quickly rehearse three short scenes, one about each syllable. But don't actually say the syllable or the word in the scene. Going back to the example of "tornado," your first scene might be about your homework assignment that your brother tore up. Your second scene might take place in a horse stable. Your third scene might be about baking cookies. The scenes need to be performed in the order of the syllables. When you are ready, perform the three scenes for the other groups, the audience, or the guesser. After you have performed all three scenes, see if they can guess what your word is.

Acting tip: You don't have to act out the syllable exactly, as long as what you're acting out sounds enough like the syllable for the guessers to figure it out. For example, if your word is "yesterday," you can act out "yes," and use the word "dirt" for "ter," and act out "day." If the guesser can figure out "yes," "dirt," "day," he can guess your word.

SUGGESTIONS FOR THREE-SYLLABLE WORDS

★ Elephants: act out the letter *L*, "love," and "fence"

★ Hypnotize: act out "hip," "note," and "eyes"

★ Telephone: act out "tell," "love," and "own"

★ Cantaloupe: act out "can," "tell," and "lobe" (as in "ear lobe")

★ Mysteries: act out "miss," "stir," and "ease"

★ Manhattan: act out "man," "hat," and "tan"

★ Paperback: act out "pay," "purr" (the sound a cat makes), and "back"

★ Porcupine: act out "pork," "you," and "pine"

 Play It Again, Sam!

Play **Pantomime Syllables**. Perform your three scenes without using words or sounds.

Act a Joke

Two or more actors

Here's an easy way to make up comedy skits that audiences are sure to enjoy. If you have access to lighting effects, a blackout (turning off all the lights in the house) is the perfect way to end these scenes. If not, ask someone to say, "Blackout," just after the punch line.

To begin, spend some time practicing telling jokes. Think of long jokes, jokes that tell stories, and jokes that involve different characters.

Choose a joke to act out. Decide who will play each character. (You can also add on to the joke so that everyone has more lines.) Decide on the blocking for the joke (see chapter 1 for more on blocking). Rehearse your joke until you are ready to perform in front of an audience.

Here's an example of how **Act a Joke** might work. The joke: Three people are driving through the desert when their car breaks down. They continue their journey on foot, traveling for days across the hot desert. Finally, they reach a palace. The sultan of the palace hears of their journey and calls them in. He says, "You three are very brave. Tell me: what did each of you bring that helped you survive in the desert?" The first person says, "I brought a large canteen filled with cold water, so we would not go thirsty." The second says, "I brought an umbrella to shield us from the hot sun." The sultan turns to the third person and asks, "What did you bring?" The third person replies, "I brought along the car door." "Why?" asks the sultan. The third traveler replies, "So when it gets too hot, I can roll down the window!"

Here is what you would act out. Madeline, Max, and Will act like they're driving in a car. They pretend that it suddenly jerks to a stop.

MADELINE:

Oh, no, our car broke down.

MAX:

We'll have to continue our journey on foot.

WILL:

But it's so hot here in the desert. We'll never make it.

MADELINE:

We have to try.

NARRATOR:

Three days later.

MADELINE:

Look up ahead. I see a castle!

MAX:

Hurray!

The term "slapstick comedy" comes from farces (comedies with highly unlikely plots) that had characters hitting each other with a wooden stick for humor. It means very broad (not subtle) comedy.

WILL:

We're saved!

MESSENGER *(entering)*:

I am a messenger of the sultan. He wants to know what you are doing at his castle.

MADELINE:

Our car broke down.

MAX:

We have traveled for days across the hot desert.

WILL:

We are very tired and hungry.

MESSENGER:

Come this way.

NARRATOR:

Later that night, in the sultan's palace . . .

SULTAN:

My messenger told me your tale. You three are very brave. Tell me: what did each of you bring that helped you survive the desert?

MADELINE:

I brought a large canteen filled with cold water, so we would not go thirsty.

MAX:

I brought an umbrella to shield us from the hot sun.

SULTAN *(to Will)*:

What did you bring?

WILL:

I brought the car door.

SULTAN:

Why?

WILL:

So when it gets too hot, I can roll down the window!

NARRATOR:

Blackout.

Commentcials...

Commercials

Be the inventor, the writer, and the star in this creative activity. Use your commercials in between scenes of your play—or, if you have access to a video camera, have someone videotape your commercials so you can see how they look on television.

Begin by talking about commercials and products people sell. Many commercials feature slogans and jingles. A "slogan" is a saying that helps you remember the product, such as, "Silly rabbit, Trix are for kids." A "jingle" is a song that does the same thing. Create your own commercial by following these steps.

1. Invent a new product. One way to do this is to think of a need or problem people commonly have and create a product that will solve this problem. For example, if you are always running out of juice, maybe you can make an invention that is part orange tree and part juice machine. It could make fresh orange juice whenever you want it.

2. Name your product. The orange tree–juice machine could be called the "Incredible Treechine."

3. Create a slogan for your product. For this combination orange tree–juice machine, how about, "With the Incredible Treechine, you'll never be thirsty again!"

4. Create a jingle for your product. Here's an example of a jingle that is sung to the tune of "The Happy Birthday Song":

    The Incredible Treechine
    Makes juice like a dream
    You'll never be thirsty
    It's the best thing you've seen.

5. Make up an entire commercial for your product using your slogan and jingle. The Incredible Treechine commercial might go like this scene, which takes place in a kitchen:

MOM:

Oh, no, we're out of juice again!

SON:

Why don't we get the Incredible Treechine?

MOM:

What is that?

SON:

It's part orange tree and part juice machine. It makes fresh orange juice whenever you want it. With the Incredible Treechine, you'll never be thirsty again.

MOM:

Let's buy one today!

MOM AND SON (singing):
The Incredible Treechine
Makes juice like a dream
You'll never be thirsty
It's the best thing you've seen.

6. Rehearse your commercial until it's ready to be performed.

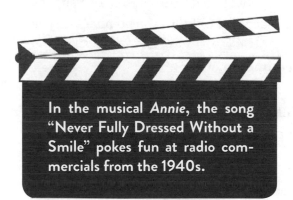

In the musical Annie, the song "Never Fully Dressed Without a Smile" pokes fun at radio commercials from the 1940s.

Chain-O-Links

This is a storytelling game that highlights the beginning, middle, and end, and it lets the players make up the in-between.

Choose one player to stand stage left facing the audience or other players. That player gets to say the beginning the story. One way of creating that is to take suggestions from the audience for an animal and an object to fill in the following blanks: "Once upon a time there was a . . . with an . . ."

Choose a second player and assign that player the lyric from a song or a famous quote. This line will be said in the middle of the story, so this player stands center stage.

Then choose a third player who will stand all the way stage right and say the end of the story. One way to do this is to take a suggestion from the audience for a place and to fill in the blank: "And the . . . was never the same."

The players each say their lines in order:

BEGINNING PLAYER:

Once upon a time, there was a chicken with an umbrella.

MIDDLE PLAYER:

Come on, everybody, it's the hamster dance.

END PLAYER:

And the popcorn factory was never the same.

Now other players have to think of sentences that might link these three together to create a story. One at a time, a player joins the line onstage and adds a sentence. Players can join anywhere in the line to add their parts of the story. They should remember what they say because it will be repeated. Every time a new sentence is added, the story is repeated including the new sentence. Continue the game until the story is complete; usually four to six sentences will be added.

Here's an example of how to play. Ryan comes up with a line to be added in between the beginning and middle players. He stands between them and the story is retold, each of them saying their original line, but adding Ryan's in order:

BEGINNING PLAYER:

Once upon a time, there was a chicken with an umbrella.

RYAN:

He didn't use the umbrella for rain; he used it for his special dance.

MIDDLE PLAYER:

Come on, everybody, it's the hamster dance.

END PLAYER:

And the popcorn factory was never the same.

Next, Molly adds to the story. She decides to stand between the middle and end players.

BEGINNING PLAYER:

Once upon a time, there was a chicken with an umbrella.

RYAN:

He didn't use the umbrella for rain; he used it for his special dance.

MIDDLE PLAYER:

Come on, everybody, it's the hamster dance.

MOLLY:

But the poor chicken didn't know the hamster dance. He only knew the umbrella dance.

END PLAYER:

And the popcorn factory was never the same.

Ian gets an idea and stands between Ryan and the middle player.

BEGINNING PLAYER:

Once upon a time, there was a chicken with an umbrella.

RYAN:

He didn't use the umbrella for rain; he used it for his special dance.

IAN:

He was very excited to show off his dance at the popcorn king's party, where the DJ said . . .

MIDDLE PLAYER:

Come on, everybody, it's the hamster dance.

MOLLY:

But the poor chicken didn't know the hamster dance. He only knew the umbrella dance.

END PLAYER:

And the popcorn factory was never the same.

Kay then stands between Molly and the end player to add her sentence to the story.

BEGINNING   MIDDLE   END

BEGINNING PLAYER:

Once upon a time, there was a chicken with an umbrella.

RYAN:

He didn't use the umbrella for rain; he used it for his special dance.

IAN:

He was very excited to show off his dance at the popcorn king's party, where the DJ said . . .

MIDDLE PLAYER:

Come on, everybody, it's the hamster dance.

MOLLY:

But the poor chicken didn't know the hamster dance. He only knew the umbrella dance.

KAY:

Luckily the other party animals were happy to learn the new dance, which unluckily required the chicken to open up his umbrella indoors.

END PLAYER:

And the popcorn factory was never the same.

Cora jumps up in between Kay and the end player to add one last sentence to the story.

BEGINNING PLAYER:

Once upon a time, there was a chicken with an umbrella.

RYAN:

He didn't use the umbrella for rain; he used it for his special dance.

IAN:

He was very excited to show off his dance at the popcorn king's party, where the DJ said . . .

MIDDLE PLAYER:

Come on, everybody, it's the hamster dance.

MOLLY:

But the poor chicken didn't know the hamster dance. He only knew the umbrella dance.

KAY:

Luckily the other party animals were happy to learn the new dance, which unluckily required the chicken to open up his umbrella in doors.

CORA:

Everyone knows opening an umbrella in doors is bad luck, and sure enough, as soon as the chicken opened his umbrella, there was a huge explosion.

END PLAYER:

And the popcorn factory was never the same.

In a World . . .

Three or more actors

The voice that announces movies always makes them sound so exciting and dramatic. There are no dull movie announcers, so there's never a dull moment in this game. Everyone works together to create the craziest movie ever!

Players stand in a circle. One player begins by stepping into the middle of the circle and saying the phrase, "In a world . . ." She completes her sentence in a way that sets up a made-up movie. As she speaks, she walks around inside the circle and ends up in front

of another player. He switches places with her and continues the movie trailer where she left off. At the end of his sentence, he gives the turn to another player in the circle. The game continues until the movie trailer is complete.

Try to remember the types of things movie trailers include, like who the stars of the movie are, who the director is, who created the music, plot details, and the line "From the people who brought you . . ." Make sure you name the movie and say when it's coming to theatres.

Here's an example of how to play:

MARK:

In a world where children are not allowed to drive cars, one child defies the rules.

ALICE:

Little Leonard will get behind the wheel, and madness will follow.

KAITLIN:

Starring Elmo as Little Leonard and Daniel Radcliffe as his wise friend, Amos.

ALPHONSO:

With music by Justin Bieber, this movie will have you laughing and crying at the same time.

MEREDITH:

Don't miss *Driving Mr. Crazy*, coming this fall to a theater near you.

Late for Work

Four actors

Bosses can sure get angry when employees are late for work. This humorous improv guessing game makes work a whole lot of fun. Choose actors to play these characters:

★ The boss

★ Two on-time employees

★ One late employee

Send the late employee out of the room and decide why he is late and how he got to work. The two should be unrelated. For example, he is late because he was attacked by clowns, and he got to work on a camel.

The boss stands center stage, and the two on-time employees stand stage left. The late employee enters and stands stage right. The boss looks at the late employee and yells, "You're late!" The late employee looks past the boss at the other two employees, who try to pantomime the reason he's late. They silently act out being attacked by clowns until the late employee tells his boss, "I was attacked by clowns." Then the boss asks, "How did you get here?" The on-time employees then pantomime riding a camel until the late employee figures it out and tells his boss.

To add to the fun, periodically the boss can turn around and catch the on-time employees in an interesting position. When the boss turns around, they must freeze and come up with a work-related reason why they are in the position they're in.

When the late employee makes a guess that is close to correct, the audience can let him know by snapping. When the late employee guesses correctly, the audience lets him know by clapping.

⭐ 6 Creating Characters

One of the most exciting things about theater is the chance to become someone else. One of the actor's most important jobs is creating and developing her character. Whether you are cast as a character in a play or are making up a character for a new scene, play, or story, it's important to give your character a life of her own. The way she talks, walks, and moves; her personal history; and even her favorite color can be important things for an actor to know about her character.

The activities in this chapter are used for character development. These activities will help you learn to commit to your character while having fun becoming someone else.

You can develop animal characters with **Duck Duck Animal** and **Poor Animal**—new takes on familiar games.

How characters stand, walk, and move is explored in **Family Portraits**, **Through the Door**, and **Body Parts**. How they talk is explored in **The Sentence Game** and **Boom Chica Boom**. You can put all these elements together in **Short Scenes**.

The activities **Visualization** and **Hot Seat** are useful to fully develop a character who is ready for a performance.

The character most often portrayed in movies is Sherlock Holmes.

Today women can play men's roles. Glenn Close played a bearded pirate in the movie *Hook*.

Duck Duck Animal

Four
or more
actors

If you like Duck Duck Goose, you'll love this version, which lets you explore animal characters as you participate in a high-speed chase. All you'll need is room to run.

Sit in a circle and choose one person to be the ducker. The ducker walks around the outside of the circle, patting everyone on his or her head as she passes and saying, "Duck." When she wants to choose someone to chase her, instead of saying "Goose," she names any animal she wants, such as an elephant. The player chosen chases her around the circle acting like an elephant, remembering to make the noise and movements of an elephant as he runs. The ducker runs safely to the elephant's place in the circle or is tagged and sits in the middle.

If tagged, the ducker remains in the middle until the next animal is caught. The elephant now becomes the ducker, but he keeps acting like an elephant as he walks around the circle, patting people on their heads. The elephant continues around the circle saying "Duck" until he chooses someone by saying another animal name, such as "Cat." The person chosen acts like a cat, and the cat then chases the elephant. Everyone else in the circle should cheer for his or her favorite animal. Continue the game until everyone has at least one chance to be the ducker.

When you're picked, act like your animal the entire time, making the sounds and movements of that animal. Remember, some animals can run faster than others; some crawl, some hop, some fly, and some swim.

Poor Animal

This game is about how funny animals can be and how hard it can be not to laugh. You can develop your animal characters and practice keeping a straight face with this game. Because it requires no setup, it's easy to play anytime, anywhere.

Sit in a circle. One player goes into the center of the circle and tells everyone what animal he will be, such as a cow. He then goes up to someone seated in the circle and acts like a cow. He makes the noise a cow makes—"moo"— three times to the seated player. The seated player looks this animal in the eyes and says, "Poor cow, poor cow, poor cow," without smiling. If the seated player smiles, she must go into the middle of the circle and become the next animal. If she doesn't smile, the animal must try to make another player smile with his mooing.

The animal continues until someone smiles. If the animal tries everyone and no one smiles, the first player who did not smile becomes the next animal. Whenever a new player takes a turn, he or she chooses a new animal.

As a young actor, Laurence Olivier—a famous stage and film Shakespearean actor—had trouble not giggling during rehearsals.

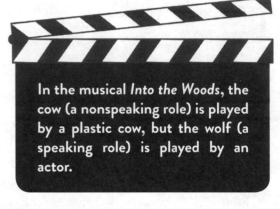

In the musical *Into the Woods*, the cow (a nonspeaking role) is played by a plastic cow, but the wolf (a speaking role) is played by an actor.

Family Portraits

Three or more actors

A picture tells a lot about a character—the way she stands, the expression on her face, the way she interacts with others. This activity gives you ideas for different kinds of characters. It's as fun to watch as it is to play. If you're playing with a group, divide in half so that half can watch while the other half plays. Then switch off.

In each group, choose one player to be the photographer. All the other players in this group get together and pose like they're having their picture taken. The first picture should look like a nice family portrait; perhaps some people are kneeling in front while others are standing in back. Once you are in position for your portrait, the photographer calls out a kind of family, such as, "The musical family." She counts to three. The posing players have three seconds to change their positions and pose the way the musical family would pose. For example, you might change the position of your arms and pretend to be playing an instrument. By the time the photographer is done counting to three, everyone should be frozen in his or her new pose.

The photographer calls out another type of family, such as, "The sleepy family," and counts to three. Again, before the photographer finishes counting to three, the posing players change their positions and facial expressions to become sleepy. The photographer calls out four family types; then the next group takes a turn.

The Sick Family

SUGGESTIONS FOR FAMILY TYPES

★ Crazy family

★ Sick family

★ Magical family

★ Loving family

★ Fighting family

★ Goofy family

★ Circus family

★ Dancing family

★ Rock and roll family

★ Gymnastics family

★ Sports family

★ Swimming family

★ Movie-star family

★ Sad family

★ Fire-fighting family

★ Artist family

★ Aerobics family

★ Lion family

★ Teacher family

Remember, you are making a picture, and pictures can't move or make sounds. Try to stay in the same place in the picture—so if you are kneeling in the front, you should always be kneeling in the front, even when the type of family changes.

 Play It Again, Sam!

If you have an audience or are playing in front of a group, have the photographer take suggestions from the audience for types of families.

Through the Door

Now that we have seen how characters pose in **Family Portraits**, the next step is to see how they walk. Everyone has a different kind of walk, and how a character walks can tell a lot about him or her. Here's a game that makes you act without any preparation time. You will need a stage or a room with a door; actors will need to be able to enter and exit through the door. The audience should not be able to see what's behind the door, but the actors should be able to hear through it.

The occupation most often portrayed in movies is a police officer.

The real person most often portrayed in movies is Napoleon Bonaparte.

Choose one player to be the director. Everyone else makes a line backstage (or out the door or behind the screen). The director should not be able to see the players and should not know their order in line. The director calls out a character. It can be a famous person or a type of worker. For example, the director may call out, "Cheerleader." The first player in line comes out and walks across the stage as a cheerleader. She may speak if she wants to, but the most important thing is to walk like a cheerleader. After she has walked across the stage, she goes back through the door and to the end of the line. The director then calls out another character, such as "Captain Hook," and the next actor in line comes out as Captain Hook, walks across the stage, and

COWBOY!

gets back in line. The game continues until everyone has played a number of characters.

This game can get humorous because the players don't know what character they will be asked to play, and the director doesn't know who is next in line. The director may call out, "Snow White," and a boy may be next. Or the director may call out, "A mouse," and the tallest person in the group may be next. The player must give his or her best performance, no matter how different the part may be to portray.

For ideas for characters, think of your favorite stories, famous people, or different types of work people perform.

SUGGESTIONS FOR CHARACTER TYPES

★ Wicked witch
★ Ballet dancer
★ Robin Hood
★ Librarian
★ Mad Hatter
★ Wrestler
★ Pinocchio
★ Scuba diver

 ## Play It Again, Sam!

Play **Reverse Through the Door**. Let each player decide what character he is performing when he comes through the door and have the director guess who he is.

Body Parts

Two
or more
actors

Here's another way to explore how different characters move. Watch other people and notice how they walk and move. Some people walk with their shoulders swinging; others walk with their chests out. For this activity, you will need room to move around.

Walk around the room. Notice the way you walk and the way others around you walk. Now walk emphasizing your head. Here, "emphasize" means to accentuate, to use the most, with the most energy. To emphasize your head, you can lead with it or move it around any way you want. Think of how it feels to walk this way. Think of what sort of character walks this way. For example, you might think that the kind of person who emphasizes her head is a very smart person. Make up a name for this character. You might call her Professor Jones. Make up what this character does for a living. Perhaps she is a scientist. When you know your body movements and feel comfortable with your expression, introduce yourself to other people in the room. Go up to someone and say, "Hello. I'm Professor Jones. I'm a scientist." After everyone has introduced herself to everyone else, quietly walk around like yourself again.

Continue this activity emphasizing other parts of your body, such as your chin, shoulders, chest, stomach, hips, or feet.

The Sentence Game

Two or more actors

The next step in developing characters is figuring out how they talk. This simple activity lets you explore the voices of different kinds of people.

Sit in a circle. Choose one player to come up with a sentence that is easy for everyone to remember. If you're working on a play, choose a line from the play.

Next, choose a character or type of person. The chooser says the line in character first; then everyone else in the circle has a turn, one at a time, going clockwise.

After everyone has had a turn, the second player in the circle comes up with a new character for the same line. After the second player performs it, each player performs it in the same order as before. Continue until everyone has at least one turn at choosing a character.

You can use this game to practice accents by picking characters from around the world, such as a Southern belle, a French chef, a cowboy, a queen, a New York cab driver, or a bullfighter.

★ Play It Again, Sam! ★

Combine **Through the Door** with **The Sentence Game**. Choose one player to be the director. He needs to come up with and tell the other players a sentence before they go backstage. When the director calls out a character, the first player in line enters, walks across the stage as the character, stops center stage, says the line in character, and then goes backstage.

Boom Chica Boom

Two or more actors

Here's a song that works like **The Sentence Game**—perfect for practicing characters and warming up your voice. There's no melody; just say it in rhythm.

LEADER:

Boom chica boom.

PLAYERS:

Boom chica boom.

LEADER:

I said a boom chica boom.

PLAYERS:

I said a boom chica boom.

LEADER:

I said a boom chica rocka chica rocka chica boom.

PLAYERS:

I said a boom chica rocka chica rocka chica boom.

LEADER:

Uh huh.

PLAYERS:

Uh huh.

LEADER:

All right.

PLAYERS:

All right.

LEADER:

One more time.

PLAYERS:

One more time.

LEADER (*choosing a character or style*):

Baby-style.

PLAYERS:

Baby-style.

Now the song is repeated, only the words are spoken in character—that is, how a baby would say them. See **Family Portraits**, **Through the Door**, and **The Sentence Game** for ideas for other styles.

Short Scenes

Three or more actors

Use this activity to see how changing characters affects a scene and how different characters act with one another.

Choose one player to be the director. Everyone else chooses a partner. With your partner, make up a short scene in which each actor says a few lines. Make the lines easy to remember—you'll have to repeat them, but you can't write them down.

Your short scene might go something like this:

THEO:	Hello.
MARIA:	Hi.
THEO:	What's in your hand?
MARIA:	Some candy.
THEO:	I love candy.
MARIA:	Do you want some?
THEO:	Sure, thanks!
MARIA:	Bye.
THEO:	Good-bye.

Now the director assigns characters to each pair of actors. In turn, each pair performs their rehearsed scene using these assigned characters. Notice how switching up the characters' relationship changes the way the scene goes. In the above scene, Maria might give Theo some candy if they are girlfriend and boyfriend, for example. But she might not if they are enemies. The director should give each pair three character assignments before the next pair performs.

SUGGESTIONS FOR CHARACTER PAIRS

★ Parent and child
★ President and reporter
★ Boss and employee
★ Monster and witch
★ Teacher and student
★ Basketball player and fan
★ Pirate and queen
★ Movie star and director

Visualization

After you've performed many different characters, it's time to settle on one character to fully develop him. This is especially important if you are playing a character in a play. Use this visualization activity to explore your character's world. This is a quiet activity where you are thinking up answers and making decisions about your character without talking out loud.

One player can read while the other players lie down on the floor on their backs. Their arms should be at their sides, their legs should be uncrossed, and their eyes should be closed. Turn out the lights. Now you're ready to begin. (The following is written imagining a female character, but you can substitute the pronouns to make it work for a male character, too.)

Think about your character. Picture your character in your head; picture what she looks like from her head to her toes. Start with her head. What color is her hair? What style is her hair? Is it messy or neat? What color are her eyes? Does she wear glasses? Imagine her face, nose, and mouth. Does she wear makeup? Does she wear earrings or a necklace?

Imagine the clothes she's wearing. What colors are her clothes? How do her clothes feel? Are they tight or loose fitting? Is your character big or small? See your character's hands. Is she wearing rings or bracelets? Does she paint her nails? Are her hands clean?

Imagine your character's feet. If she wears shoes, what kind does she wear? Does she wear socks? Are her feet big or small?

Now think about your character's life. How old is she? Does she have a family?

Does she have friends? A lot of friends or just a few close friends? Is she married? Does she have a boyfriend? Does she have any children? How does she feel about her husband or boyfriend? Her children? How does she feel about herself?

Think about her favorite things. What is her favorite color? What is her favorite food? Does she eat a lot or a little? What are her hobbies? What's her favorite sport? What's her favorite game?

Does your character work? What does she do for a living? Does she like her job?

Where does she live? Is it warm or cold? Is it a big or small town? How long has she lived there?

Now imagine that you are your character and you are sleeping in her room. Imagine all four walls of the room. What sort of things are hanging on the walls? Is the room messy or clean? What colors are in the room? Imagine all of the furniture.

Open your eyes and pretend like you're waking up, as if you are your character in your character's room. Begin getting ready for your day. Imagine there's a full-length mirror in your room. Look into the mirror as you get ready. See yourself as your character in this mirror. Notice how you look from head to toe.

When you have finished getting ready, leave your home to go wherever your character normally goes after waking up and dressing. On the way there, stop at a park. Walk around the park. See something in the park that makes you sad. Go to the thing that makes you sad. See if there is anything you can do. Continue walking around the park. Now see something that makes you happy. Go

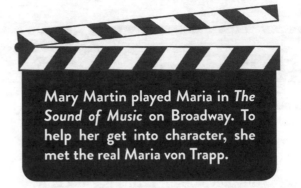

Mary Martin played Maria in *The Sound of Music* on Broadway. To help her get into character, she met the real Maria von Trapp.

to the thing that makes you happy. Leave the park and continue going where you were going. After your arrive at your destination, you may sit down.

Talk about the visualization. Everyone can share what in the park made them sad and what made them happy. Where was everyone going?

If you have time after **Visualization**, players can stay in character and continue with **Hot Seat**, the next activity. If not, players may "take off" their characters, as they would an outfit, and leave them in an imaginary safe place where these characters can be retrieved next time.

Hot Seat

Three or more actors

Once you're in character, it's time to let everyone else meet the new you.

PROP

★ A chair

To begin this game, everyone needs to put on the character he created in **Visualization** or the character he is developing for a play. Place one chair at the front of the room. Everyone sits on the floor in front of and facing the chair.

One player begins by sitting in the chair. This player is in the hot seat. One at a time, the other players ask questions of the person in the hot seat. The person in the hot seat answers these questions in character; that is, she answers the questions as the character would, giving responses that fit the character she is portraying. You can ask any questions you like. Find out as much about the character as you can. If you have done a visualization, ask her what in the park made her sad, what made her happy, and where she was going.

When everyone's questions have been answered, a new player sits in the hot seat and answers questions. Continue until everyone has had a turn in the hot seat.

Acting tip: If you're in the hot seat and someone asks you a question you're not certain how your character would answer, make up an answer. There are no wrong answers in this activity.

Oftentimes when a female actor portrays a character in a play who wears dresses, the director will tell her to bring her rehearsal skirt to rehearsals so that she can get used to walking, sitting, and acting in character.

Character Diamond

Creating characters is one of the greatest things about acting. Here's a great way to come up with original and humorous characters.

Four players stand in a diamond-shape formation facing the group or audience. The player at the point of the diamond closest to the audience strikes a pose. The other players copy the pose so that all four are standing the same way. This will be the way the character likes to stand.

The players then rotate. The new player in front makes up a voice to go along with the pose. The others copy the voice while standing in the pose. This will be the character's voice.

Players rotate again. This time the player at the point comes up with a catchphrase, or something the character likes to say. The others copy the catchphrase, saying it with the character's voice and in the character's pose.

Rotate again. Now it's time to name the character. The last person at the point creates a name for the character. All four players say, "My name is . . . ," in the character's voice and in his pose. Then they say the character's catchphrase.

Now a new character has been created! Use that character in an improv scene or sketch.

 Play It Again, Sam!

Play **Double Character Diamond**. Have two teams of four players each create a character standing in two diamonds next to each other. Then have those two characters interact in an improv scene. Rotate so that everyone who helped to create the character has a chance to play it.

Character *La Ronde*

Five or more actors

La ronde means "the round" in French. In this long-form improv game, players rotate into two person scenes. The ideas for their characters come from the two in the previous scene.

Players begin in a line facing the audience. The two players at the beginning of the line step forward. They tell the audience where the scene will take place. It should be a place where many different people who know each other gather, such as a family reunion. They

then ask the audience for suggestions for their characters. For a family reunion, they could ask two audience members to describe their strangest relative. They start a scene playing those two characters. During their scene, they talk about another family member, describing that character. The next character in line enters as the character described by the first two. Player 1 makes up a reason, in character, to leave the scene, leaving players 2 and 3 to continue a two-person scene. During their scene, they describe another relative who is at the reunion. Player 4 then enters, portraying that character. Player 2 makes up an excuse, in character, to leave the scene, and players 3 and 4 continue in a two-person scene. The game continues until all players have played a two-person scene.

SUGGESTIONS FOR LOCATIONS

★ Family reunion
★ Office party
★ School cafeteria
★ Park
★ Teacher's lounge
★ Greenroom of a theater

Here's an example of how to play. Tara, Eddie, Mia, Alex, and Katie are standing in a line facing the audience. Tara and Eddie step

forward and ask two members of the audience to each describe a relative. Based on audience suggestions, Tara will play Uncle Mark, who loves to golf and always smiles. Eddie will play Cousin Britt, who is a spy.

TARA:

Hi, Cousin Britt! Check out my golf swing.

EDDIE:

Shhh—I'm undercover.

TARA:

Oh, right. I hardly recognized you.

EDDIE:

I'm on a big case right now. I'm spying on Aunt Nancy.

TARA:

Did you hear that Aunt Nancy drives a limo now?

EDDIE:

Yes, and she's always humming a happy tune. It's very suspicious.

MIA (enters as Aunt Nancy):

Hi, Uncle Mark! Hi, Cousin Britt! Would you like to go for a ride in my limo?

TARA:

No thanks. I've got to get on the golf course. I'll see you later.

Tara exits. Mia enters, humming a happy song.

EDDIE:

That song you're humming—where did you learn it?

MIA:

I learned it from my brother, Martin.

EDDIE:

I thought so. You and Martin have been planning to take over the family band.

MIA:

How did you know?

EDDIE:

I have my ways.

MIA:

I'm not sure that I want to be in a band with Martin. He's a drummer, and he's always drumming on everything.

ALEX (enters as Martin, drumming on everything):

Hi there.

EDDIE:

I've got to go call the authorities.

Eddie exits.

MIA:

Martin, can you please stop drumming on everything for one minute!

ALEX:

> I can't! I have to drum all the time. It makes me happy.

MIA:

> Just like flowers make Mom happy.

ALEX:

> Exactly. Mom's so happy to be here in the garden that she can't stop giggling.

KATIE *(enters as Mom, giggling)*:

> Here, I picked some flowers for you.

MIA:

> Thanks, Mom. I'm going to go give these to Cousin Britt. She seems like she could use them.

Mia exits.

KATIE *(giggling)*:

> Here, son. Drum on my flowers.

ALEX:

> Sure, Mom.

The scene ends.

★ 7 ★
Improvisation

....

When you do "improvisation," you act off the top of your head. Because nothing or very little is planned in advance, no scripts are necessary, and the characters and plots come from your imagination. Sound hard? It's actually very simple and a lot of fun!

One of the things that makes improv so much fun is that anything can happen. Because there are no actual props or scenery, you can create anything simply by saying it. If your scene partner is hungry, hand them an ice-cream cone. If you're adventurous, go on a safari. The possibilities are endless.

Who, What, and Where; **The Yes Game**; **The Question Game**; and **Past, Present, and Future** will teach you the basic rules you need to know to become a successful improv actor.

The final twenty-three activities in this chapter show different ways to use your improv skills in scenes. Many involve taking suggestions from the audience—a wonderful way to get your audience involved in your scene.

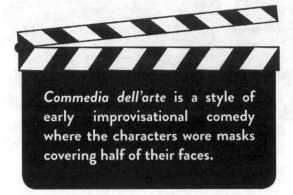

Commedia dell'arte is a style of early improvisational comedy where the characters wore masks covering half of their faces.

Who, What, and Where

You may have heard of improvisation in jazz music. In jazz, musicians improvise from a tune's melody, and what they play is influenced by the other musicians. There are definite similarities between improv acting and jazz music. Both happen without much planning in advance. The musicians know the basic melody and improvise around it. "Who," "what," and "where" form the basic melody in improv.

WHO

Who you are and what your relationship is to your scene partner(s), such as:

★ Parent and child
★ Salesperson and customer
★ Teacher and student
★ Boss and employee
★ Movie star and fan
★ Basketball player and coach

WHAT

An initial action to start the scene. It should be active, rather than just talking about something, such as:

★ Building a sand castle
★ Trying on clothes
★ Taking a test
★ Painting
★ Watching a parade
★ Learning to dribble a basketball

WHERE

Where your scene takes place, such as:

★ Beach
★ Mall
★ Classroom
★ Office
★ Street
★ Gymnasium

The Yes Game

Two or more actors

Play this game to discover the most important rule of improvisation.

With a partner, decide on a "who," "what," and "where" for a scene. Begin improvising your scene, but as you are acting with your partner, always say no to him. Say no, disagree, and negate your partner in every way. If your partner says, "Look at that elephant," you might say, "That's not an elephant—that's a rocket ship." If your partner says, "Let's go swimming," say no. Act out the "no" scene for a few minutes so that you and your partner have both had a number of chances to say no.

Now start your scene again, keeping the same "who," "what," and "where" but this time always saying yes. Agree with everything your partner says. Build on everything your partner creates in the scene. For example, this time, if your partner pretends to see an ele-

phant, you might say, "Yes, he's the biggest elephant I've ever seen!" If your partner wants to go swimming, go swimming! Act out the "yes" scene for a few minutes. Then bring it to an end.

After completing these two scenes, discuss which scene was more fun, had more action, and was more interesting. Chances are, in your "no" scene, you and your partner just stood around arguing and didn't get to do anything, while in your "yes" scene, you had the chance to do many active things. You saw an elephant, went swimming, and more.

The most important rule of improv is to always say yes. Play **The Yes Game** with your scene partner at all times. Working together in this way will make your scenes more active and much more interesting for your audience to watch. If you always remember to play **The Yes Game**, you'll be a successful improv actor.

The Question Game

Play this game to discover the second most important rule of improv.

With a scene partner, decide on a "who," "what," and "where." Begin improvising your scene, but as you're acting with your partner, you may only ask questions. You may not answer questions or make any statements of any kind, including, "I don't know."

Your scene might go something like this:

JAMAL:

What do you want to do?

SABRINA:

Do you want to go outside?

JAMAL:

Is it raining?

SABRINA:

How should I know?

Act out the question scene for a few minutes so that you and your partner both have a chance to ask a number of questions.

Now start your scene again, keeping the same "who," "what," and "where"—only this time, you may only say statements. Do not ask any questions. Also, remember to play **The Yes Game**. Act out the statement scene for a few minutes. Then bring it to an end.

After you've acted out a question scene and a statement scene, discuss which scene was better and more interesting. Chances are that your statement scene was more interesting and went further than your question scene.

The number two rule of improv is, don't ask questions. There are two reasons you should not ask questions in improv. First, you never have to ask a yes or no question because you are already playing **The Yes Game**. Asking the question just takes up time in your scene and is not active. So instead of saying, "Do you want to go swimming?" say, "Let's go swimming." Your partner will agree, and you'll be splashing around in no time. Second, asking questions puts a lot of pressure on your scene partner. For example, if you say, "What is that thing?" you force your partner to make up what it is. It's better to say, "Look at that lion!" Then your partner can talk about the lion to further develop the scene and move it along.

Past, Present, and Future

Two or more actors

Play this game to discover the third most important rule of improvisation.

With a scene partner, decide on a "who," "what," and "where." Begin improvising your scene, but as you're acting with your partner, talk only about the past or the future. Talk about what you will do tomorrow or what you did yesterday, but do not talk about what you're doing right now. Act out this past-future scene for a few minutes.

Now start your scene again, keeping the same "who," "what," and "where"—only this time, stay in the present. Instead of talking about going to the

mall, go there. Instead of talking about something you used to do, do something now. Also, remember to play **The Yes Game** and make statements, not ask questions. Act out this present scene for a few minutes. Then bring it to an end.

Once you've acted out a past-future scene and a present scene, discuss which scene was better. Chances are your present scene had more action. Active scenes are more interesting than scenes where the characters only stand around and talk.

The third most important rule of improv is to stay in the present.

Freeze

Also called **Stop and Go**, this improv game is perhaps the most famous. Two players start by choosing a line of dialogue. Then they begin to improv a scene that includes a lot of action. At any time, another player can say, "Freeze." Both actors immediately stop the scene right where it is and freeze. The person who said "Freeze" taps one of the actors on her shoulder. She leaves the scene, and the person who tapped her replaces her, taking her exact position. The new player starts a brand-new scene based on the position he is in. The other person in the scene goes along with the new scene, and the scene continues until someone outside the scene says "Freeze" again.

RULES

1. You must wait at least three lines before calling out "Freeze."

2. You must take the exact position of the person you are tapping out.

3. The person who called "Freeze" is the one who starts the new scene. The other actor must follow her lead.

4. The new scene should have nothing to do with the last scene.

Acting tip: This is an improv game, so don't plan anything in advance. When you see an interesting position, say "Freeze." Then immediately get into the same position and start a new scene.

Here's an example of how this scene might work. Christina and Victor begin a scene with, "I just love going to the circus," which is the first line of dialogue.

CHRISTINA *(jumping up and down)*:
> I just love going to the circus.

VICTOR:
> Me too. *(Pointing)* Look at that funny clown.

CHRISTINA *(standing on tip toes)*:
> I can't see. I can't see.

ROCHELLE:
> Freeze!

Cinderella and Romeo and Juliet are two plays that have been performed as ballets.

Christina freezes on her tip toes. Victor freezes pointing. Rochelle taps Victor on the shoulder. Victor steps away from the scene, and Rochelle takes his place. Rochelle starts a new scene based on Victor's pointing pose and Christina's tiptoed pose.

ROCHELLE:
You're a much better ballet dancer than that girl over there.

CHRISTINA *(pretending to do a ballet dance):*
I know, but I must keep practicing.

The new scene continues until someone calls out, "Freeze."

 Play It Again, Sam!

Play **Blind Freeze**. Blind Freeze ensures that everyone takes a turn at **Freeze** and relieves players of the pressure of deciding when to call "Freeze" and the temptation of trying to think of something in advance.

Before two actors begin the first scene in **Freeze**, a third player turns his back to them so he cannot see what the scene looks like. When the two players are in an interesting position, another player or leader says, "Freeze." The two actors freeze, and the third player turns around to see what position he has been given. He has to tap one of the two actors on the shoulder, assume their exact position, and start a brand-new scene based on the position. As he does so, the next player turns around so she cannot see the new scene. When "Freeze" is called in the new scene, that player turns to see the position and start a new scene. The game continues until everyone has had a chance to start a scene "blind."

Styles

Three or more actors

This game lets you explore many different kinds of acting and theater styles while you improvise. Two players agree on a "who," "what," and "where" and begin improvising a scene. After a moment, another player, who is not in the scene, calls out a style of acting, such as musical comedy. Without stopping the scene, the two players in the scene begin acting as if they were in a musical. After a few moments, the player outside the scene calls out a new style, such as drama. Now the players immediately begin to act like they're in a drama. Each time a new style is called, the players change their style of acting but keep the scene going. The players continue until the scene comes to an end.

You can come up with a number of different styles of acting from thinking about your favorite books, plays, and TV shows.

The word "tragedy" literally means "goat song" because the ancient Greeks put on plays in which they sacrificed goats.

SUGGESTIONS FOR STYLES

- ★ Soap opera
- ★ Science fiction (outer space) adventures
- ★ Cartoon
- ★ Tragedy
- ★ Silent (pantomime)
- ★ Sitcom (family comedy)
- ★ Opera
- ★ Talk show
- ★ Horror show

- ★ Shakespearean play
- ★ Documentary (educational)
- ★ Kung fu movie
- ★ Spy novel
- ★ Music video
- ★ Courtroom drama
- ★ Foreign film
- ★ Police drama
- ★ Farce (broad comedy)

 Play It Again, Sam!

If you're working on a play, use this game to work on your script. As the actors run through the show, the director calls out different styles. The actors continue acting out the current scene but immediately change their style of acting.

Play **Emotion Styles**. Instead of calling out acting styles, call out different emotions, such as happy, sad, scared, excited, angry, or shy. Even if you're acting out a happy scene, if "sad" is the emotion style called, make it as sad as you can without changing the lines but by changing your acting.

Who Am I?

Three or more actors

You can tell a lot about people by how others treat them. Here's an improv guessing game that puts you in someone else's shoes. The trick is to figure out whose.

One player leaves the room or goes somewhere where he can't hear the other players. These players decide on one famous person for this exited player to be. The exited player is called back into the room. When he enters the room, the scene begins with everyone treating him as if he is this famous person. Continue acting until he can guess the name of the famous person he is supposed to be. When he knows who he's supposed to be, instead of saying it, he should become the character. He lets everyone else know that he has figured out the identity of this famous person by doing things that this famous person would do. For example, instead of saying, "I'm Michael Jordan," he might start a game of basketball. Once it's clear that he has correctly identified the famous person, the scene can be brought to an end.

Continue playing until everyone has a chance to be a famous person.

Park Bench

Three or more actors

Here's a chance to play your favorite celebrity. See how long it takes for others to figure out who you are.

PROPS

★ Three chairs or a bench

Set up the chairs next to each other so they make a bench facing the audience or the rest of the group. One at a time, three players enter the room. Each acts like a famous person. They sit on the park bench and pretend to be in a park. They talk among themselves while each player tries to figure out who the other two famous people are. When one player knows the identity of another player, she lets them know while staying in character. For example, instead of saying, "You're Benjamin Franklin," you might say, "It's a good thing you discovered electricity." As soon as someone has guessed who you are, make up an excuse, in character, to leave the park. Then you may reenter as a new character.

RULES

1. There can only be three people in a scene at one time.

2. Don't say who you are.

3. Remember the three rules of improv.

Party Quirks

Four or more actors

Remembering the rules of improv while trying to figure out what's wrong with the players around you makes this game very interesting.

Choose one player to be the host of the party and send him out of the room where he can't hear you. Three people play the guests at the party, and each comes up with a quirk. A "quirk" is some peculiar or unusual trait. It can be as normal as having the chills or as crazy as having spaghetti for hair.

Call the host back into the room. The scene begins with the host getting ready for the party. One at a time the guests arrive, acting as party guests who have quirks—whatever quirk each guest came up with—added into their behavior. The host must figure out what each guest's quirk is by acting out the party scene with them. When the host thinks he knows what a guest's quirk is, he says so in character. For example, the host might say, "Would you like me to turn up the heat? I see you have the chills," or "I just love pasta—do you mind if I try a piece of your hair?"

When the host has guessed a quirk correctly, the other guests applaud, and that particular guest makes up a logical reason, in character, to leave the party. For example, the guest with spaghetti hair might say, "I have to go to the store for some tomato sauce."

The game continues until all of the quirks have been guessed correctly.

SUGGESTIONS FOR QUIRKS

★ You think you're a king or queen.
★ You sneeze jewelry.
★ You speak in opposites.
★ You have an imaginary friend.
★ You think you're a car.
★ You're magnetic.
★ You haven't slept in days.
★ Your clothes are way too small.
★ You have X-ray vision.
★ You're made of rubber.
★ Every time you lie, your nose grows.
★ You glow in the dark.
★ Every time someone says the word "yes," you cluck like a chicken.

 Play It Again, Sam!

Play **Party Quirks** in front of an audience. Take suggestions from the audience for quirks and ask the audience to applaud when the host guesses correctly.

Superheroes

Another party setting, but this time it's a gathering of crazy superheroes. One person is selected to be the host of the party, and three people are the guests. Decide on a world problem to solve, such as the tearing down of the rain forest. One at a time, the guests arrive at the party. The host greets each of them by making up a superhero name for the character and welcoming him or her. Each guest immediately creates a character based on that name and acts like that person. When all the guests have arrived, the host announces that they've been invited to the party to solve this specific world problem. While remaining in character, the players must come up with a plan to solve this problem; then the scene must be ended.

The superhero name doesn't have to be based on a real superhero. Use your imagination to think of crazy names.

In the television show *Wonder Woman*, Linda Carter frequently had to act like she was flying in an invisible airplane.

SUGGESTIONS FOR CRAZY SUPERHERO NAMES

★ Frog Girl (player must act like a frog)
★ Screamer (player must scream)
★ Opera Woman (player must sing like an opera singer)
★ Repeat Man (player must say everything twice)
★ Incredible Jumping Woman (player must jump up and down the entire time)
★ Bird Man (player must act like a bird)
★ Boneless Boy (player must pretend to have no bones)

Hidden Intentions

Three or more actors

If you've ever wanted something but been afraid to ask, you're not alone. In some plays, a character doesn't always come right out and ask for what she wants. An "intention" is what you want. In this improv game, you have to get what you want . . . without saying it.

Two players (named Paige and Antonio for this explanation) need to decide on a "who," "what," and "where" for a scene that they'll create. Paige leaves the room (or goes where she can't hear). Antonio is given an intention by a third player, Heidi—something Antonio wants from Paige, his scene partner. It can be an object, such as her hat, or an action, such as wanting her to tie his shoe. They switch places—Paige comes back into the room and Antonio leaves—and Heidi gives Paige an intention.

After both Paige and Antonio have intentions, they begin acting out their scene. Throughout the scene, each of them tries to figure out what the other player wants and gives it to them, but neither player can come right out and ask for what he or she wants. When Paige, for example, figures out what Antonio wants, she should make it part of the scene. Instead of saying, "Oh, you want my hat," Paige might say, "My hat would look much better on you. Why don't you try it on?" After both intentions have been guessed, the players bring the scene to an end.

 Play It Again, Sam!

Play **Hidden Intentions** in front of an audience. Take suggestions from the audience for the intentions and ask them to applaud when they are guessed correctly.

Double Scenes

Four or more actors

Practice the concept of give-and-take in improvisation (see **Give-and-Take** on page 56). It's important to know when to give focus to the other scene and when to take focus back.

Divide into two groups. Both groups chose a "who," "what," and "where" that are somehow related, such as a husband and wife picking out furniture at the furniture store and two painters who are painting the couple's home. Both groups set up their scenes next to each other. One group begins improvising. They continue for a few moments, until the other group takes focus by beginning their scene. The first group gives them the focus by freezing in whatever position they are in. The second group acts out their scene until the first group takes focus again, and the second group freezes. This continues until both scenes come to an end.

This game can get very funny because you can use what you hear in the other scene. For example, hearing that the painters are painting the house

THIS COUCH WILL LOOK GREAT WITH OUR NEW CARPET

light blue and yellow, the actors playing the husband and wife could pick out furniture that is bright green and purple.

SUGGESTIONS FOR RELATED "WHO," "WHAT," AND "WHERE" SCENES

★ A mom and dad eating dinner at a restaurant; a baby and babysitter finger painting at home

★ Two wives shopping for their husbands at a mall; two husbands shopping for their wives at a mall

★ A dentist giving a dental exam to a patient in his office; another patient and a nurse filling out forms in the waiting room

★ Two friends decorating for a party at the birthday girl's house; the birthday girl and another friend listening to music in a car parked outside the house

OOOPS!

The Storytelling Game

Three or more actors

The oldest-known playwrights used narrators to tell their stories. You can use this activity as a writing tool as well as an improv game. It will give you a lot of ideas for stories and characters.

To see how to create a play in the style of story theater from **The Storytelling Game**, read the scenes "The Tale of Jeremy Fisher" and "The North Wind and the Sun" found in chapter 11.

PROP

★ A chair

Set up a chair on one side of the stage or playing space, facing the audience. Choose someone to sit in the chair. This person is the narrator or storyteller. She begins telling a story that she makes up as she goes along. The other players act out the story as the narrator tells it. These players become whatever characters or objects the storyteller needs for her story and provide all the sound effects. Remember to give and take.

The story that has been remade the most times in plays, movies, and television shows is *Cinderella*.

The narrator needs to pause from time to time while telling the story so that the other players can act out the scene she has just described. During her pauses, the other players take the focus and act out that part of the story. Then they freeze and return the focus to the narrator to hear the next part of the story.

Try to play this game without planning anything in advance, including who will play each part. When a narrator mentions a character, a player immediately jumps in to become that character. Play **The Yes Game** so you are not arguing over the parts.

...AND THEN HE STARTED MOWING THE LAWN.

Here's an example of how this game might work.

NARRATOR:
> Once upon a time there was a duck.

One actor immediately jumps in and becomes the duck.

DUCK:
> Quack!

NARRATOR:
> The duck lived in a pond.

The other players make the sounds of a pond.

NARRATOR:
> One day the duck noticed his reflection in the water.

One player jumps in to become the reflection.

DUCK:
> Oh, look! My reflection.

NARRATOR:
> He didn't like what he saw.

DUCK:
> I look terrible.

NARRATOR:
> So he went to the duck beauty parlor.

Players who were the pond now create a beauty parlor.

NARRATOR:
> A beautician gave the duck a feather cut.

One player becomes the beautician.

BEAUTICIAN (*cutting Duck's feathers*):
> Snip, snip. There you go.

NARRATOR:
> The beautician told the duck to sit under the dryer for a while.

BEAUTICIAN:
> Go sit under that dryer.

One player becomes the dryer.

NARRATOR:
> After a few minutes, the duck was ready to go.

DUCK:
> Thanks a lot! I'll see you later.

NARRATOR:
> And when he looked in his reflection this time, he liked what he saw.

The same player that acted as the reflection becomes the reflection again.

DUCK:
> Much better.

NARRATOR:
> The end.

The Dubbing Game

Four or more actors

In order to understand what the actors are saying in foreign films, sometimes their voices are dubbed over so it sounds like they are speaking English, even though their lips look like they are speaking another language. When films are "dubbed," the original sound is removed so the new sound can be added. This game lets you be the actors and the dubbed voices.

Choose two people to be the actors and two to be their voices. The players begin by agreeing on a "who," "what," and "where." Each voice player stands near his actor player. The actors

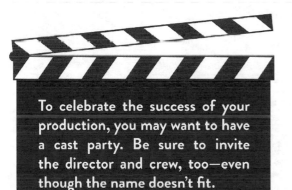

To celebrate the success of your production, you may want to have a cast party. Be sure to invite the director and crew, too—even though the name doesn't fit.

begin improvising the scene—they don't talk, but they move their lips as if they are talking. When the scene begins, the voice players begin speaking for the actors. Remember to play **The Yes Game** in the scene so that the voices go with the movements. For example, the voice should not say how sleepy the character is while the actor is jumping up and down.

Play this game at least twice so each player can be an actor and a voice.

In this game, both the actors and the voices have power. The actors have the power of movement. No matter how they move, the voices must play **The Yes Game** and make it work with the lines. The voices have the power of speech. No matter what they say, the actors must play **The Yes Game** to make it work with the movements. You can make a successful improv scene when you work together.

Gibberish

Two
or more
actors

"Talking gibberish" means mumbling or creating your own language, with sounds and words that you make up. Try having a conversation with someone in gibberish. See if you can understand each other by the way you say things—the "emphasis" that you place on each word—rather than the actual words you say. After you have practiced speaking gibberish, try this improv scene.

Choose a partner and agree on a "who," "what," and "where." Your scene should involve teaching others how to do or make something. Give the title of your scene before you perform it. It should be in the form "how to . . ."; for example, "how to bake cookies." Decide who will speak gibberish and who will "interpret," or restate what the other is saying in English. Do not plan anything else in advance. Begin your scene with the person speaking gibberish explaining how to bake cookies, pausing every couple of sentences so the interpreter can restate what's being said in English. Play **The Yes Game** so that the English translation goes with the gibberish. Continue the scene until you have finished explaining how to bake cookies.

ZOOBLE MOOG JUMBY GOOGLEE

SUGGESTIONS FOR HOW-TO SCENES

★ How to tie your shoe
★ How to swim
★ How to ride a bicycle
★ How to make a peanut butter and jelly sandwich
★ How to change a light bulb
★ How to change a tire
★ How to fix a broken doll

 ## Play It Again, Sam!

Play **Gibberish**, but this time the interpreter doesn't speak. Instead, she acts out what the other player is saying in gibberish.

Slide Show

Three or more actors

If you've ever sat through a slide show of someone else's vacation, you know how boring it can be. Here's a way to make it very interesting.

One person is the presenter; everyone else is part of the slide show. The presenter begins telling the story of his vacation. Throughout the story, the presenter says, "Next slide, please." The other players strike poses to look like people in a photo from a vacation. The presenter uses this group pose to tell a story. The players keep their poses, as if they are an actual slide, until the presenter says, "Next slide, please." Then the players change their poses, and the presenter continues the story of his vacation, explaining this new pose as if it were the very next slide from his vacation.

The presenter can set up how the players will pose by saying something like, "In my next slide, you will see us climbing the mountain. Next slide, please." The players pose as if they are climbing a mountain. Or the presenter can let the players create a picture on their own by giving the next slide no introduction. In this case, the presenter must somehow work this new pose into the story. Continue the scene until the presenter has finished the story of his vacation.

Keyword

Three or more actors

Here's an improv scene with a twist to keep you on your feet. In a group, choose a "who," "what," and "where." Each player in the group chooses a word—such as "snake," "bus," or "together"—that is related to the "who," "what," and "where" chosen. Begin improvising your scene. Whenever your word is said, if you are onstage, exit, and if you are offstage, enter. (If you're not playing on a stage, leave the scene and reenter the scene when your word is said.) You must exit and enter in character. Be sure to make up a good reason to exit or enter each time your word is said. You can have a lot of fun sending your scene partners in and out by working their words into the scene, but don't forget, they can do the same to you. Continue with the game until your scene comes to an end.

Here's an example of how this game might work. Eve's word is "snake," Jake's word is "bus," and Connor's word is "together." Their "who," "what," and "where" is three friends making cookies in a kitchen.

EVE:

I can't wait to eat all of the cookies we're baking.

JAKE:

Me too, and I'm so glad we could all get together for once.

CONNOR:

Oh, no, we're out of sugar. I'll go borrow some from next door.

Connor exits because the word "together" was said.

JAKE:

Let's cut the cookies into shapes.

EVE:

Great idea. I'll make mine shaped like a bus.

JAKE:

I'd better go see what's taking our friend so long with the sugar.

Jake exits because "bus" was said.

EVE (*calling offstage*):

Hurry up, you guys! I thought we were baking together!

Connor reenters because "together" was said.

CONNOR:

Well, they didn't have any sugar, but they showed me their cool new pet snake.

EVE:

Look at the time. I've got to go catch my bus. See you later.

Eve exits because "snake" was said. Jake reenters because "bus" was said.

JAKE:

No sugar. Oh, well, so much for making cookies. I guess we'll try again tomorrow.

The scene ends.

The Alphabet Game

Here's an improv scene with a challenging twist that will make you think before you speak.

With a scene partner, choose a "who," "what," and "where." The first line of your scene must start with the letter *A*, the second line of your scene must start with the letter *B*, and so on throughout the alphabet. Each line must start with the next letter of the alphabet. If you have trouble remembering where you are and if you have a third player, you can have him or her call out the next letter after each line of dialogue. Your scene should end when you get to the letter *Z*.

Here's an example of how this game might work. The "who," "what," and "where" is two zookeepers cleaning a cage at the zoo.

KELSEY:

All night we have to clean, clean, clean.

JORDAN:

Boy, you said it.

KELSEY:

Cages smell like animals.

JORDAN:

Don't even think about it.

KELSEY:

Elephants smell the worst.

JORDAN:

Forget about the smell. Let's get to work.

KELSEY:

Great, the ape's cage is almost finished.

JORDAN:

Hope they don't wake up while we're in here.

KELSEY:

I have to finish scrubbing the floor.

JORDAN:

Just do it quietly or they'll wake up.

KELSEY:

Kind of scary being in here at night.

JORDAN:

Listen to that monkey snore.

KELSEY:

My, he's filthy—let's clean him.

JORDAN:

Nobody said we had to clean the monkeys.

KELSEY:

Of course not, but he's so dirty.

JORDAN:

Perhaps if we just give him a little shower.

KELSEY:

Quietly turn on the hose.

JORDAN (*turning on the hose*):

Ready—it's on.

KELSEY:

Splash water on him.

JORDAN (*showering the monkey*):

That's better—now he's clean.

KELSEY (*pointing*):

Up there is a monkey walking across the rope.

JORDAN:

Very hard for that monkey to keep her balance.

KELSEY:

Wonder what happens if she falls.

JORDAN:

X-rays will be needed.

KELSEY:

Yes, we'd better call for help.

JORDAN:

Zebra cage can wait until later.

The scene ends.

Name Yes

This is a great name-learning game that also helps teach the improv concept of **The Yes Game**. The most important thing to know in this game is that you are not allowed to move from your spot in the circle until another player has said "yes" to you, thus giving you permission to move.

Players stand in a circle. One player (Eloise) starts by pointing to another player and saying his name (Greg). That player says "yes" to her. Eloise can then leave her spot in the circle and start walking towards Greg's spot. Before she gets there, Greg needs to point to another player and say his name (Sean). Greg can't move out of the way for Eloise to have his space until Sean says "yes" to him. Sean says "yes," and Greg begins walking toward Sean's place in the circle. Sean then must say someone else's name to get another space before Greg gets there, and so on.

After a while, the game should flow smoothly so that players are walking into spaces as other players are leaving them.

 Play It Again, Sam!

Once names are learned, play this game as a word-association game. Players can say any word they want when they point to another player. The most important part is that the other player always answers with "yes."

Best Field Trip Ever!

Two or more actors

Here's another way to discover the magic of **Yes And**. An entire room of people can play this game at the same time; then they tell each other about the field trip they have planned.

Sit with a partner and begin planning the best field trip ever. But every sentence you say must start with either "No" or "Yes, but." For example, player 1 may say, "Let's go to Hawaii," and player 2 responds with, "No, it's too expensive," or "Yes, but not during the summer." Continue the conversation for about three minutes, remembering to start every sentence with "No" or "Yes, but."

Then share with the group what plans you made. Chances are you didn't even reach a decision on where to go, much less plan the best field trip ever. Now start the conversation over again, but this time every sentence must start with, "Yes, and." You're not allowed to say "no" or "but." Plan the best field trip ever with your partner, and start each sentence with, "Yes, and." Notice how much further you get in your planning and how much more positive and fun the field trip is. Share the field trip you created with the group.

"Yes And" Monster

Three or more actors

Now that you know the most important rule of improv, here's a game that will demonstrate just how fun and creative **Yes And** can be.

Players sit in a circle and imagine that there is a monster in the middle of the circle. One player starts by making a statement about the monster, such as, "That monster has bright green fur." The player to her left says, "Yes." Then he repeats the previous statement and adds "and": "That monster has bright green fur, and." He then adds another statement about the monster, such as, "She's wearing a frilly pink dress." The next player says, "Yes," repeats the previous statement, says "and," and adds another fact about the monster. Make sure you always say, "Yes, and." "No" and "but" are not allowed in this game. Continue the game until everyone has had a chance to add at least one piece of information about the monster. Then talk about what an amazing monster you all created together. Individually, this specific monster could never have been created. It took a group of improvisers playing the **Yes And** game to make it happen.

OTHER "YES AND" THINGS YOU CAN CREATE TOGETHER:

* ★ An alien
* ★ A sandwich
* ★ Soup
* ★ A dollhouse
* ★ A swamp
* ★ An ant colony

Better Letters

Two actors

If you're having trouble taking too fast, this game is sure to slow you down. It also sounds very silly and will have you or your audience laughing in no time.

Two players choose a "who" and "where" (or take suggestions from an audience). They are then told that, in their scene, they must replace every *S* with a *T*. They improvise their scene, but as they talk, every word that has an *S* in it, is said with a *T* instead.

Here's an example of how to play. Lee and Erin have chosen to play a doctor and a patient in the doctor's office.

ERIN:

What teems to be the problem?

LEE:

Well, Doctor, I'm tick.

ERIN:

Doet your tomach hurt?

LEE:

Yet. And to does my note.

ERIN:

Your note? What happened to your note?

LEE:

I trained it.

 ## Play It Again, Sam!

Try other combinations of replacing letters, such as *B* for *N*, and *W* for *T*.

Countdown

Five actors

This game is as exciting as rocket ship blasting off! The actors have to remember the order of scenes so they can revisit them in backwards order.

Player 1 starts a scene alone onstage doing something that someone could do alone, such as playing hopscotch. After a few moments, player 2 enters and starts a completely different scene, such as working at an ice cream parlor. The two actors continue that scene for a bit until player 3 enters and starts a brand-new scene. He might say, "Welcome to your first day of yoga." Players 1 and 2 act out the yoga class for a few moments until player 4 enters and starts a brand new four-person scene, perhaps in preschool. They all play the preschool scene until player 5 enters and starts something new altogether, such as a baseball game. After a few moments of playing baseball, player 5 makes up an excuse in character and leaves the scene. The other four actors immediately go back to the fourth scene, the preschool. Then player 4 makes an exit from that scene, and the three immediately return to the yoga class. In a few moments, player 3 exits that scene, and the two remaining actors return to the ice cream parlor. Then player 2 exits the scene, leaving player 1 alone onstage playing hopscotch.

10 - 9 - 8 - 6 - 7 - 5 - 4 - 3 - 1 - 2

Old Job, New Job

Imagine if a firefighter suddenly decided to become a dentist. He might get the two careers mixed up. This game explores the craziness that would ensue if that were to happen.

Choose one or two players to be the customers . . . or victims. It depends on the situation, whether you want the first one or the second one. For example, the dentists only need one patient, but the waiters could use two customers. Then choose two other actors to play the workers. Tell them what their old job was and what their new job is. Have them improvise a scene exploring all the ways that could get crazy.

EXAMPLES

★ Old job: firefighters; new job: dentists. The dentists may try to examine the patient's mouth with a hose.

★ Old job: dog trainers; new job: waiters. The waiters may give the customers treats for good behavior.

★ Old job: carpenters; new job: hairstylists. The hairstylists may try to cut hair with a saw.

Gibberish Interpreter

Speaking gibberish is a great actor's tool, because it puts the focus on physicality, tone, and emotion. This game heightens emotions in a heated debate.

Three actors stand onstage facing the audience. The actor in the middle is the interpreter. The other two will have a debate in gibberish. Imagine that the interpreter speaks both languages and can interpret for each one what the other said. They are given a suggestion of a topic to debate about, such as whether hot dogs or hamburgers are better. Stage-right actor begins by making a statement in gibberish. The interpreter tells the stage-left actor in English what the other actor said. Stage-left actor responds in gibberish, and the interpreter tells the stage-right actor what he said in English.

The interpreter should do the best she can to interpret what the actors are trying to say by taking into account their actions and gestures. In turn, the actors should always act *exactly* like whatever the interpreter says to act like.

Five-Sided Dice

Six actors

This is a guessing gibberish game that is as fun for the audience as it is for the players.

Send one player out of the room. She will be the guesser. Five other players line up in front of the audience. Player 1 steps forward and is given a suggestion for a famous person, living or dead, to portray. Player 2 then joins player 1. The two of them get a suggestion for a famous pair or duo. Player 3 joins them, and the three of them are given a suggestion of a very famous movie. Player 4 joins the other three, and they get a suggestion for a famous landmark or tourist attraction. Player 5 joins the group and is given a suggestion for a historical event.

The guesser enters the room and begins improvising a scene. She speaks only in gibberish with player 1, who is acting like the suggested celebrity. They play a scene together for a few moments while the guesser is trying to figure out who the celebrity is. Then player 2 enters, and players 1 and 2 become the famous pair. The guesser continues in a gibberish scene with them as she tries to figure out who they are. After a few moments of that scene, player 3 enters, and the three players begin acting out the famous movie—in gibberish, of course. The guesser plays along with the scene while trying to figure out the move. Then player 4 enters, and the four actors become or act out the tour-

ist attraction along with the guesser. And finally, player 5 enters, and the five actors act out the historical event. Someone calls out, "Scene," and the guesser tells the audience who or what she thought each scene was about.

It's OK to guess wrong in this game. In fact, it adds to the humor of the scene when the guesser thinks she was in *The Wizard of Oz* when actually she was in *The Lord of the Rings*.

Clue

Three actors

The board game Clue ends with someone figuring out who committed the murder, what room the murderer was in, and what weapon he or she committed the murder with. Based on the board game, this gibberish improv game becomes a mad mystery.

Send actors 1 and 2 out of the room. With actor 3, decide on an occupation or a celebrity (the "who"), an object that was used as a weapon (the "what"), and a location or room (the "where"). Actor 1 reenters and begins acting out a gibberish scene with actor 3 in which actor 3 is pretending to be the celebrity. The scene continues long enough for actor 1 to get a good idea of who the celebrity might be. Then actor 3 begins demonstrating his surroundings and showing what kind of room he is in. He continues to talk with actor 1 in gibberish until he thinks actor 1 may know the room. Then he pretends to pick up the suggested object. He uses it and talks in gibberish to communicate what the object is. When actor 1 thinks she knows what the object is, she kills actor 3 with it. Actor 3 remains dead on the ground as actor 2 enters. This time, actor 1's job is to communicate

through the gibberish scenes the "who," "what," and "where" to actor 2. At the end, actor 2 kills actor 1 with the weapon and tells the audience what his guesses are. Then actor 1 gets up and tells the audience what her guesses were. Then actor 3 gets up and tells the first two what they actually were.

Here's a sample of play: Peter, Dale, and Rose are playing. Dale and Rose leave the room. Peter gets the following suggestions: Barack Obama in the library with a turtle.

Dale enters and begins a gibberish scene with Peter in which Peter is acting like Barack Obama. After a few moments, Peter begins to pretend to pull books off of shelves and read them. Then Peter picks up an imaginary turtle and plays with it. When Dale has a guess for what Peter is playing with, he takes it from Peter and hits him over the head with it. Peter falls down.

Rose enters. Rose and Dale begin a scene in gibberish, but Dale thinks he is Abraham Lincoln. He plays Lincoln, speaking gibberish with Rose for a few moments. Then he shows Rose that he is in a library (Dale guessed that one correctly). Next, Dale picks up a snake. When Rose guesses that the snake is a rope, she strangles Dale with it. Rose tells the audience, "It was George Washington in the library with a rope." Dale gets up and says, "It was Abraham Lincoln in the library with a snake." Peter gets up and lets them know, "It was Barack Obama in the library with a turtle."

Using and Becoming Objects

In chapter 6, "Creating Characters," you learned how to become many different kinds of animals and people. In this chapter, you can learn how to become objects. Things that aren't alive, such as furniture and musical instruments, are brought to life in **My Morning**, **Use or Become**, and **Human Orchestra**.

You can also use your imagination to find many different uses for everyday objects when you are acting. **The Object Game**, **Someone Else's Hands**, and **Scarves** are activities that let you explore objects in new ways.

Becoming objects—sometimes called "object transformation"—and using objects in new ways expands creativity both onstage and offstage.

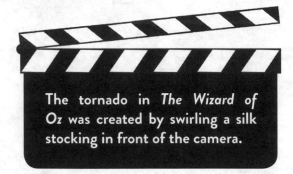

The tornado in *The Wizard of Oz* was created by swirling a silk stocking in front of the camera.

In the play *You're a Good Man, Charlie Brown*, Snoopy pretends his dog house is a fighting jet plane.

My Morning

Use your body to create everyday objects. Put them all together for an unusual and interesting scene. This activity works best with a large group, but players in smaller groups can play more than one object.

Talk about the objects in a bedroom, such as furniture, windows, and doors. Each player decides on one object in the bedroom she would like to play. (Larger objects may be played by more than one player.) After everyone has chosen an object, one player goes up to every other player and uses it. For example, if someone is a window, "open up" that person. If someone is the bed, lie down on him or her. Do the same thing with the bathroom, the kitchen, and the living room.

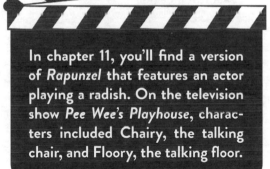

In chapter 11, you'll find a version of *Rapunzel* that features an actor playing a radish. On the television show *Pee Wee's Playhouse*, characters included Chairy, the talking chair, and Floory, the talking floor.

Once you've created and practiced each room, put them all together in a story entitled "My Morning." Start by having everyone recreate the bedroom objects again. Wake up in your bed with your alarm clock going off. Turn off your alarm clock and gather your clothes for the day. Continue getting ready, but be sure to use all of the objects in the bedroom. Next, go to the bathroom. Everyone quickly recreates his or her object in the bathroom. Look in the mirror and brush your teeth. Take a bath or shower and get dressed. Use all of the objects in the bathroom. Next, go to the kitchen. Everyone quickly recreates his or her object in the kitchen. The storyteller can make breakfast and sit at the kitchen table. Try and use all the kitchen appliances while making breakfast so that everyone has a chance to perform. Finally, go to the living room. Sit on a chair or couch and read a book or listen to music. Use all of the living room objects. Then bring the story of your morning to an end.

Play this game a few times so a couple of players can act out their mornings.

Use or Become

Two or more actors

Become an object or use pantomime (see chapter 9) in this fast-paced activity.

Choose one person to be the object caller. Everyone else begins the game by walking around the room. The caller names an object. The walking players have two choices—they may either use the object or become the object. They must do so immediately, without pausing. As soon as everyone is using or has become the object, the caller tells the group to walk around again. After a few seconds, the caller needs to name another object for the other players to use or become.

Continue the activity until everyone has used or become a number of different objects.

SUGGESTIONS FOR OBJECTS TO USE OR BECOME

★ Washing machine
★ Guitar
★ Computer
★ Light bulb
★ Camera
★ Motorcycle
★ Napkin
★ Scissors
★ Vacuum cleaner

  Play It Again, Sam!

Play **Partner Use or Become**. All the players walk around the room on their own, but when an object is called, each player must immediately match up with a partner. For each pair, one player must become the object and the other one must use it.

Human Orchestra

Four or more actors

In this game, you can become instruments and create a full symphony using only your body and your voice. This game is similar to **Conduct a Story**.

Choose one person to be the conductor. Everyone else chooses an instrument that he or she will become. Once everyone has selected an imaginary instrument, all the orchestra members gather together. They all must be able to see the conductor; some can stand in back, and others can sit in front.

The conductor begins by warming everyone up. The conductor lifts her arms, and all the players warm up by making the sounds of their instruments, as if they are tuning up real instruments. As each player makes the sound of his instrument, he also moves his body in the way the instrument moves when it is played. When the conductor lowers her arms, everyone must stop tuning up. Now the concert is ready to begin.

The conductor creates a symphony by pointing to different instruments at different times and signaling when the instruments should get louder or softer. The concert continues until the conductor brings it to an end.

You may decide on a song to play before starting the concert, or you can make it up as you go.

★ Play It Again, Sam! ★

Play **Partner Human Orchestra**. In this game, everyone must choose a partner. In pairs, one player is the instrument while the other is the musician. Play this version at least twice so that each player can act in both roles.

The Object Game

Three or more actors

When you look at a hairbrush, do you see a microphone? This competitive game has you using everyday objects in unusual ways.

PROPS

★ Three or more everyday objects

Choose one person to be the judge. The remaining players divide into two groups, team A and team B. The two teams stand across from each other and turn their backs to the judge. The judge places an everyday object in the middle of the two groups. She then claps her hands to let the two teams know they may turn around.

As soon as they turn around, a player from team A runs to the object and uses it in a way that it is not usually used. For example, if the object is a wooden spoon, he might use it as

Comedy sports involves improvisational teams competing against each other.

a guitar. The judge tries to guess how the player is using the object. As soon as the judge guesses correctly, that player runs back to his team, and a player from team B runs to the object. She uses it in a different way, such pretending to brush her teeth with it. As soon as the judge says "toothbrush," this player runs back to her team. Then team A takes a turn again. The game continues with the same object until one team cannot come up with a new use for the object. When this happens, the other team is declared the winner of that round. Play at least three rounds with three different objects.

RULES

1. No pausing. As soon as team A is done, it's team B's turn.

2. No repeating. Once an object has been used as a hairbrush, for example, it cannot be used as a brush or comb of any kind.

3. Do a good job at using the object. If the judge cannot tell what you are using it as after a few seconds, your team loses the round.

Someone Else's Hands

Three actors

In this game, one person is chosen to be the actor, and another person is chosen to be the actor's hands.

PROPS

★ Table

★ Objects that can be used near the hands and face, such as a newspaper, glass of water, hairbrush, lipstick, gum, telephone, or pen and paper

The actor stands in front of a table with various objects on it. He puts his hands behind his back. The other player stands behind him so that she cannot see the table. She extends her arms out so that her arms look like they belong to the actor in front of her.

By working together, they act out a scene using each of the objects on the table. The actor responds with words and facial expressions to whatever the second actor does with her hands. The hands respond to whatever the actor says. For example, if the hands are opening up the newspaper, the actor might say, "I wonder what's in the news today." If the actor says, "I'm thirsty," the hands might reach for the glass of water. The scene can get pretty silly as the hands try to bring the glass of water to the actor's lips, because the hands cannot see where his lips are.

Continue performing the scene for your audience until each object has been used at least once. Then, let the third player be the actor or the hands while one of the previous players watches.

Scarves

See how you can use fabric to create characters in this activity.

PROPS

★ One sheer scarf or similar type of material for each actor

Every player but one takes a scarf. The one player without a scarf will be the character caller.

To begin, the caller assigns a character to each one of the other players. Each player then uses his or her scarf to become that character. After each player is in character for a few minutes, the caller gives each player another character.

SUGGESTIONS FOR CHARACTERS CREATED WITH SCARVES

★ Ghost
★ Bird
★ Old woman
★ Superhero
★ Bride
★ Ninja
★ Bat
★ Mermaid
★ Wind
★ Airplane
★ Cocoon and butterfly
★ Little Red Riding Hood

Alien Objects

Imagine what aliens would think of Earth objects. This science-fiction game combines object creativity with a little bit of gibberish.

Players stand in a circle and imagine that they are all from the same planet and have come to Earth together to see how earthlings live. A leader puts an everyday Earth object, such as a hairbrush, in the middle of the circle. The aliens take a moment to gaze at the object in awe. Then one alien picks it up and announces, in gibberish (their alien language), what he thinks the earthlings use it for. Then he demonstrates with the object. In complete agreement, all other aliens repeat the gibberish word he called it and pretend to use one as well. Then the object is passed to the person on his left.

She comes up with another possible use for the object. She names it in gibberish and uses it. The others follow suit. The game continues until everyone has created a new word and use for the object.

Here's a sample of play: Judith, David, and Marta are playing. Judith picks up the hairbrush and calls it a "blooberflash." David and Marta agree and say, "Ah! A blooberflash." Judith uses the hairbrush as a microphone and hums into it. The others join her with pretend microphones. Judith passes the hairbrush to David.

David says, "Sipzip." Marta and Judith say, "Ah! Sipzip." David uses the hairbrush as a paintbrush, and Marta and Judith follow his lead. David passes the hairbrush to Marta. Marta says, "A cottycot." David and Judith say, "Oh! A cottycot!" Marta pretends to use the hairbrush as a spoon. The others join in.

Try That On for Size

Two actors or two teams of actors

This is a physical game that requires no preparation—just your imagination.

Two players stand next to each other facing the audience. Player 1 begins pantomiming an action, such as dribbling a basketball. Player two does the same motion.

Player 1 says, "I'm dribbling a basketball; try that on for size."

Player 2 continues the dribbling motion but tries to think of something else she could be doing that has a similar motion. She says, "I'm petting a dog; try that on for size."

The game continues back and forth with the players coming up with as many different ideas for what they could be doing with that action until one of the players can't think of one, repeats one that's already been said, or pauses too long. The other player is the winner.

 ## Play It Again, Sam!

Have two teams of actors line up. When a player is out, one of his teammates jumps in his place and begins a new action.

Play **Try That On for Size** in front of an audience. Take an audience suggestion for the action.

Gift Giving

Two or more actors

Everyone loves to receive gifts! This game shows how to be in agreement with your scene partner through object work.

Everyone sits in a circle. Choose one player to go first. He picks up an imaginary present that is wrapped. He is careful to show everyone the size and shape of the gift. Then he hands it to the person on his left.

She then opens the imaginary present and says, "Thank you for the . . ." She fills in the blank with what she imagines she has been given.

The objective of the game is to justify the shape and size of the package with the gift. For example,

if Jonathan gives Barb a small box, she may say, "Thank you for the beautiful bracelet," rather than, "Thank you for the giraffe." The gift giver should always act as if whatever the receiver said is exactly what was given. For example, Jonathan can't say, "That's not a bracelet; it's a spider."

This game is a wonderful, simple way to demonstrate the Yes Game in a scenic way. The giver gets to decide the size, shape, and weight of the gift. The receiver gets to name the gift, accepting and heightening what the giver created. The giver then agrees with the receiver, making a believable mini–improv scene.

What's in the Box?

This game lets each player use his imagination while also practicing object work.

Players sit in a circle. Each player reaches behind her, gets a great big imaginary box, and places it in front of her.

Everyone chants, "What's in the box? What's in the box? What? What? What's in the box?"

The leader calls on a player to say what she imagines is in her box, such as a kitten.

Everyone pretends to take a kitten out of his or her box and hold it, saying, "I've got a kitten; do you have a kitten? I've got a kitten!"

Then the game repeats. "What's in the box? What's in the box? What? What? What's in the box?"

The leader says, "What's in your box, Nicole?"

Nicole says, "A brain!"

Everyone takes a brain out of his or her box and holds it. "I've got a brain; do you have a brain? I've got a brain!"

★ Play It Again, Sam! ★

You can add a memory component to the game. After the game has been played, put everything back into the box. Try to remember in reverse order all the things you imagined were in the box.

Hidden Objects

Two actors

This is a two-person scenic improv game that shows how funny using imaginary objects can be.

Write on index cards the names of different objects—use one card for each object. This can be done by the group or prepared in advance. If you are playing this game for an audience, take audience suggestions for the objects. Be creative, and make sure there are a variety of objects—the stranger the better!

Choose six cards at random, without looking at what objects are written on them. Place the cards face down at various places on the stage or playing area.

Choose two players and decide on a location they can be exploring.

SOME SUGGESTIONS FOR OBJECTS

★ Aspirin
★ Blood
★ Chains
★ Crab
★ Disco ball
★ Fungus
★ Hairballs
★ Handcuffs
★ Head lice
★ Kilt
★ Mannequin
★ Mixed nuts

★ Mustache
★ Mummy
★ Pearl necklace
★ Rabbit
★ Scab
★ Screwdriver
★ Spam
★ Trombone
★ Turkey
★ Underwear
★ Whale

SOME IDEAS FOR LOCATIONS:

★ Boss's office

★ Brother's room

★ Grandma's attic

★ Hotel room

★ Pet store

★ Warehouse

The players begin improvising their scene. When they pretend to open a box, a drawer, a closet door, or anything else that can be opened, they turn over a card and pretend that whatever is written on the card is what they found there.

Here's a sample of play: Wendy and Betsy are exploring their brother's room.

WENDY:

Let's see what's under his bed.

BETSY:

OK. *(She turns over a card that says "Crab.")*

WENDY AND BETSY:

A crab!

BETSY:

Oh my gosh! A live crab under our brother's bed!

WENDY:

I'm not surprised. He's usually so crabby in the morning.

BETSY:

I'm afraid to see what's in his closet.

WENDY:

I'll look. *(She pretends to open closet door and turns over another card that says "Trombone.")*

WENDY AND BETSY:

A trombone!

BETSY:

So that's the noise we've been hearing from this room.

The scene continues until all six cards have been turned over, revealing six different objects in their brother's room.

The players should always say the object out loud right away so that the audience knows what they have discovered. Then they can react to their discovery and try to make it part of the scene.

Creative Drama

9

Creative drama means using dramatic skills and tools—such as pantomime, puppets, and masks—to create stories, scenes, characters, and plays.

"Pantomime" is a type of acting where you perform without speaking. A "mime" uses her body and facial expressions when she acts, but she does not use her voice. **New York, New York**; **Statue Maker**; and **What Are You Doing?** are games using pantomime.

For centuries, puppets and masks have been used as creative drama tools. You can create your own puppets and masks and use them in scenes. When you put on a puppet show, your hand becomes the character, and you use different voices to create different people. Use your homemade puppets in **The Frog Prince**.

When you act with masks, you use your body, because the mask never changes its expression. For example, the mask cannot smile, but you can show happiness by jumping up and down joyfully. The mask cannot cry, but you can show sadness by making your body droop.

Get your imagination in full gear for these timeless, creative drama activities.

Masks date back to ancient Japan. The samurai used masks to frighten their enemies. Primitive people used masks in rituals to earn luck, to bring rain, and to help win wars. The ancient Greeks were the first to use masks in theater.

Pantomime

One or more actors

"Mimes" are actors who do not use words or sounds when they act. They rely on their gestures and expressions to show their feelings and let the audience know what they are doing. "Pantomime" is acting without words or sounds. In improv, objects are usually pantomimed because you never know what you will need. Pantomime gives you the freedom to create any object in the world.

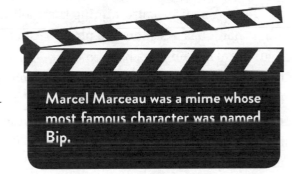

Marcel Marceau was a mime whose most famous character was named Bip.

PROPS

★ Variety of household objects (a fork, a phone, a computer, a doll, a toy car, a shovel and pail, a ball, or a mop)

Practice using your objects. Notice how your hands and body move. After some practice, perform for others without any of the objects, but move your body as you would when using each one. See if other actors can guess what object you're using.

Try acting out the following pantomime scenes alone or with a group:

★ Tug-of-war game
★ Volleyball game
★ Baking a cake
★ Working in an office
★ Playing in a sandbox
★ Cleaning a kitchen
★ Walking a dog

See how many scenes you can come up with on your own. After performing a few scenes, let another player perform while you try to figure out what he's doing.

New York, New York

Here's a fast-paced, competitive game using pantomime. All you need is room to run.

Divide into two teams. Team A goes to one end of the room, touching the wall; team B goes to the other end of the room, touching the opposite wall. Team A thinks of a job to pantomime. When team A has decided on a job, they let team B know they are ready for the game to begin.

Members of team B take a giant step toward the center and ask, "Where are you from?"

Members of team A take a giant step toward the center and answer, "New York, New York."

Members of team B, taking another giant step, ask, "What's your trade?"

Members of team A, taking another giant step, answer, "Lemonade."

Members of team B take one more step and demand, "Show us if you're not afraid."

Team A begins pantomiming their job. Team B guesses out loud what that job is. As soon as a player from team B guesses correctly, team A turns and runs back to their wall while team B runs after them, trying to tag them. If a team A member is tagged before he reaches the wall, he must join team B. The game continues with team B, coming up with a job and following the steps above until they get to pantomime their chosen job. Keep playing the game until everyone is on the same team.

Statue Maker

In this game, you can be a shopper, a salesperson, and even a magic statue that comes to life. Use pantomime to show what kind of statue you are.

Collectively decide who will be the statue maker and who will be the shopper. Everyone else will be a statue. When ready, the statue maker says, "Go crazy!" Each statue begins to dance around, moving and shaking her body every which way until the statue maker yells, "Freeze!" All statues freeze immediately.

At this point, the shopper comes in to buy a statue. The statue maker welcomes the shopper to the statue store and shows him around. They stop at each statue and turn it on, one at a time, by touching the statue on one shoulder. When a statue is turned on, it begins moving and acting like whatever kind of statue it is. As soon as the statue maker and the shopper can tell what kind of statue it is, they turn it off by touching its shoulder again. Then they move on to the next statue.

After they have checked out all of the statues, the shopper chooses which one he wants to buy. The chosen statue becomes the next statue maker. The previous statue maker becomes the next shopper. And the original shopper becomes a statue. Now the game is ready to begin again.

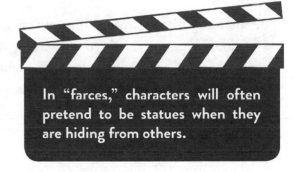

In "farces," characters will often pretend to be statues when they are hiding from others.

Acting tips for statues: When you're a statue and you're in your frozen position, think about what kind of statue you will be when you are turned on. Use the position you're frozen in to help come up with ideas for this. For example, if you freeze while lying face down on your stomach, you may want to become a snake statue or a swimming statue; if you freeze standing up with your arms in a circle above your head, you may want to become a ballerina statue or a basketball-hoop statue.

What Are You Doing?

This competitive pantomime game is for quick thinkers. Choose a partner. Ask your partner, "What are you doing?" Your partner responds with something she is not doing, such as, "I'm eating an ice-cream cone." You start pantomiming eating an ice-cream cone. Your partner asks you, "What are you doing?" Still eating the ice-cream cone, you respond with something you are not doing, such as, "I'm climbing a tree." Your partner pantomimes climbing a tree. Whatever she answers, you do. Whatever you answer, she does. The game continues until someone is out.

RULES

1. No pausing. As soon as your partner asks what you are doing, answer. If you wait too long, you're out.

2. Don't answer your partner's question with anything similar to what you are pantomiming. For example, if you're pretending to read a book, don't answer "I'm reading a book." Don't even answer, "I'm reading a newspaper." If you answer something too close to what you're doing, you're out.

3. Don't repeat. If you say something that has already been said, you're out.

Here's an example of how this game might work.

TREVOR:

> What are you doing?

APRIL:

> I'm walking a dog.

Trevor pantomimes walking a dog.

APRIL:

> What are you doing?

TREVOR *(still walking a dog)*:

> I'm making a sandwich.

April pantomimes making a sandwich.

TREVOR *(still walking a dog)*:

> What are you doing?

APRIL *(still making a sandwich)*:

> I'm taking a nap.

Trevor pantomimes taking a nap.

APRIL *(still making a sandwich)*:

> What are you doing?

TREVOR *(still taking a nap)*:

> I'm sleeping.

Trevor is out because sleeping is too similar to taking a nap. April wins the game.

Stick Puppets

One or more actors

PROPS

* Popsicle sticks (one for each puppet)
* Glue
* 1- or 2-inch Styrofoam balls (one for each puppet)
* Pieces of fabric, approximately 5 by 5 inches (one for each puppet)
* Decorating supplies, such as buttons, feathers, yarn, and sequins

Place the piece of fabric on a flat surface. Place the Popsicle stick on the fabric so that one end of the stick is in the center of the fabric and the other end hangs over the edge of the fabric. Fold the other half of the fabric over the stick and push the end of the stick with the fabric on it halfway into a Styrofoam ball. This ball will be the head of your puppet. Glue decorations on to the ball to create the eyes, ears, nose, mouth, and hair for your puppet. When the glue dries, you are ready to play with your puppet!

Hold your puppet by the bottom end of the stick. Come up with a skit or use one of the activities in the last chapter of this book and use your puppets as the performers.

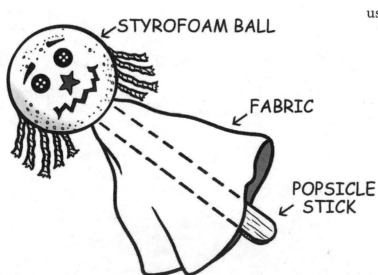

STYROFOAM BALL

FABRIC

POPSICLE STICK

Paper-Bag Puppets

One or more actors

PROPS

★ Lunch-size paper bags (one for each puppet)
★ Markers
★ Different-colored construction paper
★ Scissors
★ Glue
★ Yarn

Place the bag flat on top of a table with the flap side up. Use the flap as the mouth for your puppet. Use a marker to draw on lips—one lip above the flap and one lip below it, but connected at the flap. Cut out eyes, a nose, and ears from the construction paper. Glue these onto the bag above the flap. Use the markers to draw on more details, such as eyebrows, or cut out more shapes from the construction paper and glue them on, too. If you want, and if it suits your pup-

pet character, cut out a tongue and teeth to glue under the flap.

You can make hair for your puppet using yarn. Wrap the yarn around your arm, from your palm to your elbow, five to seven times. Cut the yarn loops at your palm and at your elbow and glue the strings to the outside edge of the bag. Allow the glue to dry completely.

To use the puppet, place your hand inside the bag and use your fingers to open and close the flap. You're ready to perform as soon as you decide on a "who," "what," and "where."

You can make shadow puppets by using a flashlight and making shapes with your hands.

 Play It Again, Sam!

Cut out a body shape and glue it below the mouth of your puppet. Now you can make your puppets sit on a bench or on your lap while you perform a skit.

Puppet Show

PROPS

★ One puppet theater (like a piano bench and enough material to drape over it to cover the front, or one large box, such as one for a refrigerator or stove, with a large square cut out from one side of the box's opening for the stage)

After you've made puppets (see the two previous activities), make up names for each of them and decide what kind of characters you've created. Are they happy puppets? Are they sad or mean? Create a voice for each puppet that suits its look. Practice talking with this voice while using the puppet. Next, introduce your puppets to everyone else's puppets. Let them interact for a while. (This will help you with the next step.)

Divide into groups of two or more. Each group should make up a story that includes all of the puppets in the group. Rehearse the show until you are ready to perform. When everyone is ready, perform your puppet shows for each other. Kneel behind the piano bench, or crouch down inside the box. Reach up high enough so that the audience can see your puppets. Remember to always move the puppet that is talking so the audience can tell which one it is.

The Frog Prince

Three to four actors

Here's a puppet play adapted from a Brothers Grimm story. You can use your paper bag or stick puppets to tell this tale.

CHARACTERS

★ Witch
★ Princess
★ Frog
★ Prince

PROPS

★ Ball
★ Two dinner plates

SCENE 1: AT THE POND

The witch puppet appears first.

WITCH:

Hello. I am a witch, and I love to turn princes into frogs! Do you want to know how I do it? I just dance my magic dance while singing, "Bibbily, babbily, boobily, bog! Turn this prince into a frog! Bibbily, babbily, boobily, boo! Until a princess kisses you." Someone's coming! I'll hide over here. *(Witch puppet hides; prince puppet appears.)*

PRINCE:

I'm lost. Have you seen anyone around here?

AUDIENCE:

A witch!

PRINCE:

A witch? Which way did she go? *(Looks left; witch appears right.)*

WITCH:

Hello.

PRINCE *(jumps)*:

Oh, hello. I didn't see you there.

WITCH:

Who are you?

PRINCE:

I am the Prince.

WITCH:

Perfect! *(Dances.)* Bibbily, babbily, boobily, bog! Turn this prince into a frog! Bibbily, babbily, boobily, boo! Until a princess kisses you. *(Prince puppet disappears, as frog puppet appears. Witch laughs and exits.)*

FROG:

> Oh dear, ribbit. I don't feel quite myself, ribbit. What's happened to me? Ribbit.

AUDIENCE:

> You're a frog!

FROG:

> A frog, ribbit! Oh, no, ribbit! *(Princess sings from offstage.)* Someone's coming, ribbit! *(Frog disappears; Princess puppet appears with ball.)*

PRINCESS *(singing)*:

> Oh, what a day to play and play with my ball of gold, truly beautiful to behold. *(Drops her ball into the pond.)* Oh, no! My beautiful ball of gold! It's gone! *(She cries. Frog appears.)*

FROG:

> What's the matter, ribbit?

PRINCESS:

> My beautiful ball of gold has fallen into the pond. *(Continues to cry.)*

FROG:

> If I get it for you, may I eat, ribbit, and sleep, ribbit, in your castle, ribbit?

PRINCESS:

> Oh, yes.

FROG:

> I'll be right back, ribbit. *(Exits; then enters with the ball.)*

PRINCESS:

> Thank you! *(Exits.)*

FROG:

> Wait, ribbit! What about our deal, ribbit? *(Exits.)*

SCENE 2: IN THE PALACE

The princess puppet appears.

PRINCESS:

> The royal chef has made my favorite meal. Mmm, delicious.

FROG *(entering)*:

> Hello, ribbit.

PRINCESS:

> What are you doing here?

FROG:

> Did you forget our deal, ribbit? I came to eat in the castle, ribbit.

PRINCESS:

> A frog eat with a princess? Never!

FROG:

> But you gave me your word, ribbit.

PRINCESS:

> Very well. Here you are. *(Hands him a plate. They eat.)*

FROG:

That was delicious, ribbit. Now, where will I sleep, ribbit?

PRINCESS:

Outside with the other frogs.

FROG:

No, princess, ribbit. You promised I could eat, ribbit, and sleep, ribbit in your castle, ribbit.

PRINCESS:

Very well. My room is this way. *(She drags him up to her room.)* You can sleep there. *(They go to sleep. Prince puppet appears in a dream.)*

PRINCE:

Princess, I am not really a frog. I am a prince. An evil witch cast a spell on me. *(Prince puppet exits; witch puppet enters.)*

WITCH:

Bibbily, babbily, boobily, bog! Turn this prince into a frog! Bibbily, babbily, boobily, boo! Until a princess kisses you. *(Witch puppet exits.)*

PRINCESS *(awakening)***:**

I had the strangest dream. There was a handsome prince and a witch who said that the prince will be a frog until he is kissed by a princess. Well, it's worth a try. *(Princess kisses frog. Frog puppet disappears; prince puppet appears.)*

PRINCE:

Thank you, Princess. You have lifted the curse.

PRINCESS:

And I have learned to always keep my word. Shall we be friends?

PRINCE:

Yes.

PRINCESS:

Let's go out and play with my ball of gold.

PRINCE AND PRINCESS *(singing)***:**

Oh, what a day to play and play with my ball of gold, truly beautiful to behold.

The scene ends.

At your library, you can find other books with puppet plays, such as *Plays for Young Puppeteers* by Lewis Mahlmann and David Cadwalader Jones.

Paper-Plate Masks

One or more actors

PROPS

- ★ Paper plates (one for each mask)
- ★ Colored markers
- ★ Scissors
- ★ Yarn
- ★ Glue
- ★ Decorating supplies such as buttons, feathers, sequins, and pompons

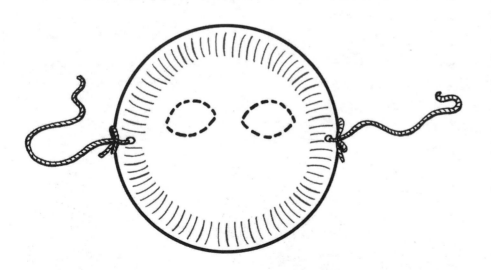

Hold a paper plate up to your face, feel where your eyes are through the plate, and use a marker to mark your eyes on the plate. Following these marks, cut out holes where your eyes will be. Decorate your mask using the markers and supplies. Be creative. Eyelashes can be made out of sequins; the ears can be made of pompons. Think about the kind of character you'd like to create and decorate your mask to fit this character.

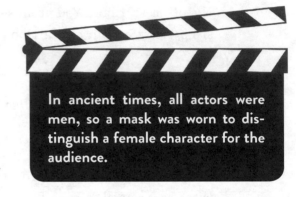

In ancient times, all actors were men, so a mask was worn to distinguish a female character for the audience.

When you're finished decorating your mask, cut one slit on each side of the plate just below your glued-on ears, about a half inch long and a half inch from the side edges of the plate. Cut two pieces of yarn, each about an arm's length, and thread one piece of yarn through each hole and knot it. Then tie the mask behind your head.

Now you're ready to perform. All you need to do is decide on a "who," "what," and "where" and find an audience; then you're ready to be onstage!

Papier-Mâché Masks

Two or more actors

Instead of a typical mask, which goes over your face, this mask sits on top of your head like a hat. Because the face of this mask will be turned toward the ceiling, you can portray two characters. When you act with this mask, tilt your head down to let the audience see the mask's face.

You'll need a partner to help you make this one.

PROPS

★ Newspaper
★ Masking tape
★ Papier-mâché
★ Large bowl
★ Scissors
★ Tempera paints
★ Paintbrushes

Place five full-size pieces of newspaper on your head. Hold the newspaper down over your ears while your partner runs a strip of masking tape all the way around the newspaper a couple of times, just above your ears—just like where the brim of a hat would be. Your partner should put enough tape on the newspaper so that it will stay in the shape of your head when you take the newspaper off. After you lift the mask off of your head, put crumpled up newspaper underneath the mask so that it won't smash down flat while you work on building its face.

Build the shape of a face on your mask by taping more crumpled newspaper on top of it to make the nose, ears, and so on. Once the mask is in the shape you want, place the papier-mâché in a bowl and follow the package directions to mix. Cut some newspaper into long strips. Dip one strip at a time into the papier-mâché mix and cover your mask with them. Cover your entire mask at least twice with the papier-mâché strips. Let your mask dry overnight.

Once your mask is dry, paint it with tempera paints. Your mask should look like a hat. You don't need to cut eye holes in this mask since you'll be wearing it on your head. When you wear the mask on top of your head, the mask's face should be looking at the ceiling. Now you're ready to get onstage.

Acting with Masks

Perhaps the most ancient form of theater, mask acting uses the body to express feelings.

PROPS

★ Homemade masks (see previous activities in this chapter)

After you have made your masks, think about the character type each one is. Create names for each inspired by these characteristics. Create a special movement for each mask character. For example, some characters might do a little dance as they walk; others might flap their arms. Put the mask on and practice moving while wearing it. After a few minutes, take turns introducing your mask to the other actors. They can introduce their masks to you, too.

Divide into groups. In your group, make up a story that includes all of the mask characters in the group. Turn the story into a scene. Rehearse the scene until you're ready to perform it. When every group is finished rehearsing, perform your mask scene for the other groups and watch the other groups' scenes. Remember to use your entire body to express how your character is feeling in your scene.

Ice Wizard

Five or more actors

This is an imaginative large-group game that combines acting with a freeze dance.

One player is chosen to be the wizard. The wizard decides what she will turn the others into—monkeys, for example. With a wave of the wizard's imaginary wand, all others become monkeys and explore the space while walking and sounding like monkeys. Then the wizard waves her wand again and freezes all the monkeys. The other players must freeze right where they are. The wizard then walks around throughout all the frozen monkeys. If the wizard isn't looking, the monkeys can try to tag the wizard, but if the wizard catches a monkey moving, she melts him with a wave of her wand. That monkey then melts to the floor and stays there until the next round. The game continues until one of the monkeys manages to tag the wizard before she sees him move. That player is then the next wizard.

Suggestion: You may want to turn the lights off and on when the wizard waves her wand. This will ensure that everyone knows when it has happened.

SUGGESTIONS FOR WHAT THE WIZARD MAY TURN THE CLASS INTO:

★ Animals, such as lions, puppies, or lizards
★ Occupations, such as dancers, basketball players, or firefighters
★ Soldiers
★ Robots
★ Aliens
★ Marionettes
★ Mermaids
★ Kings and queens
★ Leprechauns

Behind the Scenes

10

During a play, you see only the actors, but many important things happen behind the scenes.

One important job is making the sound effects for a play. For example, if the play is outside, you might use birds, wind, or car sound effects. Indoor sound effects might be needed, too, such as doorbells or telephones. You can practice these in **Sound-Effects Story**.

The audience can tell a lot about a character from his costume and makeup. Create new characters based on costumes in **Creative Costume Play**. If you're playing an animal character in a play, you can make the ears and tails with **Animal Costumes**.

Face painting is fun to do at home, at costume parties, or for plays. Use the same tools and techniques as a professional makeup artist in **Stage Makeup** and **Makeup Morgue**.

Next, try your hand at designing a set with **Sketch a Set** and **Set Diorama**. Both activities involve attending a production meeting where designers and directors meet to discuss the backstage elements of a play.

Many plays call for props or objects to be carried onstage by actors. **Prop Characters** and **Prop Scenes** will help you be creative with objects.

Once you combine the previous acting games with these backstage activities, you'll know just about everything necessary to mount a full production.

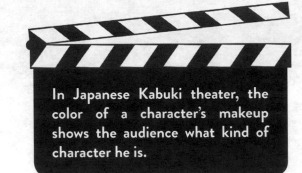

In Japanese Kabuki theater, the color of a character's makeup shows the audience what kind of character he is.

Sound-Effects Story

Though many sound effects are made with machines and instruments in movies, you can make most of these sounds by using just your voice, your hands, or your body. If you have a computer or cell phone with recording capabilities, tape this activity so you can hear what the sound effects sound like.

Choose one player to be the leader. The leader sits facing all the other players. He calls out a series of sound effects. After each one, the other players make this sound by using their voices, hands, or bodies.

SUGGESTIONS FOR SOUND EFFECTS

- ★ Alarm clock
- ★ Yawn
- ★ Shower
- ★ Opening door
- ★ Opening dresser drawer
- ★ Birds singing
- ★ Light breeze
- ★ Train
- ★ Blowing wind
- ★ Rain
- ★ Thunderstorm
- ★ Galloping horse
- ★ Stairs creaking
- ★ Doorbell
- ★ Door slamming shut

- ★ Cat
- ★ Witch laughing
- ★ Ghost
- ★ Monster
- ★ Running down stairs
- ★ Motorcycle
- ★ Babbling brook
- ★ Frog
- ★ Cricket
- ★ Splash
- ★ Blow-dryer
- ★ Popcorn popping
- ★ Crackling fireplace
- ★ Snoring

The leader reads the following story that uses these sound effects. The leader should pause after each bolded word so that the other players can make this sound.

This is the story of my scary day. I woke up to the sound of my **alarm clock**. I **yawned** and got out of bed. I took a **shower**. When I was done, I **opened up my closet door** and took out some of my clothes for the day. Then I **opened my dresser drawer** and took out the rest of my clothes and got dressed. I went downstairs and opened the front door. It was a beautiful day. There was a **light breeze** and **birds were singing**.

Off in the distance, I heard a **train coming**. The sound grew **louder** and **louder**. I ran to the train and hopped on. I rode for a while until **it suddenly stopped**. I got off the train. The **wind was blowing**. It started to **rain** a little, then **harder** and **harder**. It turned into a **thunderstorm**.

Off in the distance, I heard a **horse galloping**. The sound got **louder** and **louder**. I followed the horse to a spooky-looking house.

I walked up the **creaky stairs** and rang the **doorbell**. The **door opened** by itself. I walked inside, and the **door slammed** behind me. I **walked upstairs** very slowly. Suddenly, something jumped out at me, but it was only a **cat**. I **opened the door** of the first room. I thought I heard a **witch laughing**.

A drum is often used to make the sound of thunder for a play.

The sound grew **louder** and **louder**. I **closed the door**. I **opened the door** to the next room. I thought I heard a **ghost**. The sound grew **louder** and **louder**. I **closed the door**. I **opened the door** to the next room. I thought I heard a **monster**. The sound grew **louder** and **louder**. I **closed the door** and **ran down the stairs** and outside.

A human being makes the sound effects between scenes and before commercial breaks on the television show *Home Improvement*. One person creates the sounds of tools, animals, slamming doors, and more.

I heard a **motorcycle** coming. It **screeched** to a stop. My mom was on it. She had been looking for me. I told her about the spooky house. She said I needed to hop on the back of the bike so she could take me to the park. She drove to a **babbling brook**. There were **frogs** and **crickets** along the banks of the brook. While I was peering down at them, I lost my balance and fell off the bike and into the brook with a **splash**.

My mom took me home and dried me off with a **blow-dryer**. We **popped popcorn** and sat by the **crackling fireplace** until I **fell asleep**.

The end.

Creative Costume Play

Four or more actors

PROPS

★ Various items of clothing and costume pieces, such as scarves, dresses, gowns, jackets, ties, hats, robes, wings, animal ears and tails, gloves, and eyeglasses

★ A large box

Fill a box with various clothing items. They can be unusual and shouldn't fit just one character. For example, a cape is a good item—but it cannot be Batman's cape, because then it can only be used for a scene with Batman.

Once all the costume items are in the box, players should take a few minutes to explore its contents. Players can try items of clothing on until each player has created a costume that he likes. Now players walk around in their costumes while thinking about and eventually creating a walk that fits their costumed characters. Once every player has decided on her costume and walk, she walks around and introduces herself to each player as her new character.

After this mini rehearsal, divide into groups and make up a story that includes all of the costume characters in the group. Turn the story into a scene and rehearse it until you are ready to perform. When everyone is ready, perform your scenes for each other.

If you would like to further develop your costume characters see **Visualization** and **Hot Seat** in chapter 6.

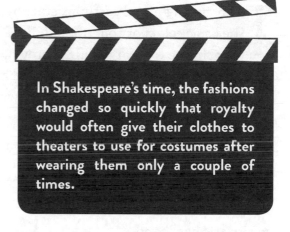

In Shakespeare's time, the fashions changed so quickly that royalty would often give their clothes to theaters to use for costumes after wearing them only a couple of times.

Animal Costumes

One
or more
actors

To create an animal costume, start by wearing clothing that has the basic colors of your animal. For example, if you are a cat, you may choose to wear all black, brown, gray, white, or orange. The only other things you need are ears and a tail.

Here's a simple way to make your own ears and tail.

PROPS
★ Construction paper
★ Pencil
★ Scissors
★ Plastic headband
★ Tape or glue
★ Socks
★ Newspaper
★ Safety pin

To make your ears, draw your ear shapes on construction paper. Cut them out, leaving a little extra paper at the bottom of each ear. Wrap the extra paper around a plastic headband, and tape or glue it on. (If you use tape, it will be easy to reuse the headband after you are done.)

To make your tail, find a sock that is the same color as your animal. Stuff it with newspapers and safety pin it to your clothes.

See the next activity, **Stage Makeup**, to complete your character's look with face painting.

Stage Makeup

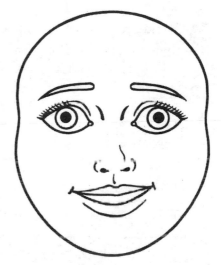

One or more actors

You can create many different characters with makeup.

PROPS

★ Makeup base (color dependent on character)
★ Black or brown eyeliner pencils
★ Rouge (color dependent on character)
★ Lipstick (color dependent on character)

Once you've chosen a character, create a makeup plan for her. You can create a makeup plan by tracing the face pattern on the following page and using makeup on the paper to design your stage face. For most of your theatrical makeup needs, you can use women's cosmetics. For special colors (such as bases for animal characters), a local costume shop or theatrical supply store are your best bets.

Choose your stage makeup colors carefully. Stage lights make everyone look pale, and in a theater, you need to be seen easily from a distance, so make them darker than normal. Design your stage face, and try out your makeup techniques at home before your performance. Standing in a room with very bright light, with full makeup on, will help you judge if you've applied enough makeup.

Here are some makeup design tips:

★ Old age: Use a darker than normal base and black or brown makeup pencil to draw in the horizontal lines that come with old age on the forehead and around the eyes.
★ Youth: Even young people need to wear a light base, rouge, and lipstick onstage so they don't look pale. This is true for both male and female characters.
★ Glamour: A glamorous woman might wear a lot of eye makeup, bright rouge, and bright lipstick. She might wear nail polish, too, if you have time to put it on.
★ Animals: Find and study a photograph of your animal. Notice the colors and lines on the animal's face. Try to recreate this look by using makeup pencils and a colored base.

In *The Wizard of Oz*, the actor who was first cast to play the Tin Man, Buddy Ebsen, had to quit because he was allergic to the silver makeup. Jack Haley is the actor who replaced him.

Makeup Morgue

A "makeup morgue" is a book that makeup designers use to help them create makeup plans for characters.

PROPS

★ Pen
★ Magazines
★ Paper
★ Scissors
★ Glue

Begin by labeling seven different pieces of paper with the following headings: "Old Age," "Youth," "Glamorous," "Animals," "Hair," "Facial Hair," and "Unusual Characters."

Laurence Olivier liked to use stage makeup to make his nose look larger for many of his dramatic characters.

Look through magazines and cut out pictures of people who depict your seven different categories. For your "Old Age" page, find pictures of older people; for "Youth," find pictures of babies, kids, or young adults; for "Glamorous," look for models and pictures of wealthy or elegantly dressed people. "Animals" can include real animals or cartoons. Look for pictures that show unusual hairstyles for the "Hair" category. For "Facial Hair," find pictures of men with beards or mustaches. For your "Unusual Characters" page, look for people who are out of the ordinary, such as superheroes, cartoon humans, elves, or space aliens. Glue the pictures onto the appropriate page. See if you can fill up an entire page for each category.

Sketch a Set

Four or more actors

The "set" is the scenery or background for a play. Before a set designer builds a set, he draws sketches of it to see how it will look. While every stage is different, many have a "backdrop"—a long back wall or a large piece of cloth painted with scenery. A backdrop may also have two "flats," which are two smaller, flat pieces of scenery placed on the stage. A stage where the audience is on only one side is called a "proscenium stage." Sketch a set design for a proscenium stage.

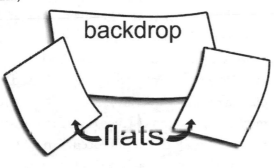

PROPS

* A piece of 4-by-10-inch white paper
* Two pieces of 4-by-4-inch white paper
* Colored pencils

Divide into teams of two or more actors. Choose a play or story and discuss the surroundings that are depicted in this play. Think about colors that would help create the mood of this play. For example, if the play is a comedy, you might choose bright, happy colors. If the play is a drama, you might choose darker colors.

Using your colored pencils, sketch your backdrop on the long piece of paper and the two flats on the shorter pieces, using one piece for each flat.

When all the groups have finished, hold a production meeting. A production meeting is a meeting where the designers explain their designs to the director and other designers. In turn, every group presents its design and explains what everything means and why they chose their colors.

To continue your set design, use your sketch to create a set diorama (see the following activity for how to do this).

The movie *Oklahoma* was actually filmed in Arizona.

Set Diorama

One or more actors

After the director and designer have agreed on the set sketch, the set designer then makes a model of the entire set.

PROPS

★ A shoe box (one for each diorama)
★ Two pieces of 4-by-4-inch cardboard
★ Glue
★ Craft materials, such as cotton balls, popsicle sticks, clay, rocks, sticks, and pipe cleaners
★ Doll-house furniture (pieces depend on play)

Set your shoe box lengthwise on a table, with the open part facing you. Glue your backdrop to the back of your box. Glue your "flats" onto cardboard so they are sturdy. You can get your cardboard flats to stand by sticking a ball of clay to the bottom edge of each cardboard piece, then flattening it on a tabletop. Place one flat on either side of your shoebox backdrop, angled out so the audience can see them once the entire set is built. Now add the furniture or other set pieces to your diorama. (What pieces you need are determined by the play script you've selected. If, for example, the entire play takes place outside, you won't need any furniture, but you might want to make trees out of small sticks or snow out of cotton balls. But if all the action occurs in a living room, then you'll need a couch and some chairs. Read through the script to pick out the furniture you'll need. This is also a great way to create a props list.)

If a number of people have created dioramas, hold a joint production meeting. Here you can show them your work and explain the choices you made; they can do the same for you.

GLUE

Prop Characters

A "prop" is anything an actor carries onstage. You can tell a lot about a character by the things she carries around.

PROPS

★ A variety of objects, such as a tea cup, stuffed animal, cellular phone, framed photo, whistle, feather, jump rope, briefcase, magnifying glass, and paintbrush

★ A large box

Place all the props you've collected into the box. All the players should examine the objects in the box; then each player picks out one that he'd like to use for this game. Next, each player needs to think about the kind of person who would carry or use this object for a prop and create a character based on this prop. Each should come up with a name, a walk, and a voice for his character. Once everyone has created a character, all players walk around, in character, and introduce themselves to the other players.

Divide into groups and make up a story that includes all of the characters and props in the group. Turn the story into a scene, and rehearse the scene until you are ready to perform. When everyone is ready, perform your scenes for each other.

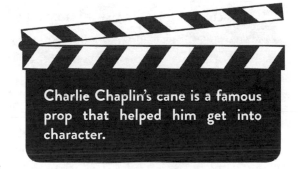

Charlie Chaplin's cane is a famous prop that helped him get into character.

In early rehearsals, the shape of the set may be marked on the floor with masking tape so the actors can rehearse moving around the scenery once it is built and placed onstage.

Prop Scenes

Two or more actors

Props can be very important, not only to characters but to the entire scene. Create scenes based on props.

PROPS

★ A variety of objects, such as a book, an umbrella, a tea pot, a potted plant, a framed photo, a hanger, a whistle, a feather, a basketball, a jump rope, a yo-yo, a briefcase, a magnifying glass, a cookie cutter, and a pair of glasses

Divide into groups. Each group selects three objects that have nothing to do with each other—such as a hanger, a basketball, and a cookie cutter—and creates a scene about the three objects by coming up with a "who," "what," and "where." Rehearse the scene until you're ready to perform. When each group is ready, perform your scenes for each other.

 ## Play It Again, Sam!

Have one person select three objects from the box that no one chose the first time around. In turn, each group can create a scene using these three props. See how different each of the scenes turns out. After every group has gone, discuss the different ways the props were used in each scene.

Monologues, Scenes, and Plays

If you like to work with a script rather than creating your own play, you have thousands of scripts to choose from. Your library will have many books containing plays for young people to perform. (See "Suggested Plays and Stories for Kids" on page 223 for some specific titles.)

If you're performing alone, try acting out a monologue. A "monologue" is a scene in which one actor speaks aloud to himself, to another character, or to the audience. This chapter includes monologues from **Rip van Winkle**, **The Snow Queen**, and **Alice in**

Wonderland. You can find other monologues in plays and in books of monologues, or you can create one for yourself. For small groups of actors, there are two scenes in this chapter—*The Tale of Jeremy Fisher* and *The North Wind and the Sun*—that were created by professional children's theater actors using the **Storytelling Game** from chapter 7.

For a challenge, you can perform theater classics that offer comedy and drama. A scene from a classic British comedy, *The Importance of Being Earnest*, gives two female actors the chance to speak with British accents.

The first scene of an original version of *Rapunzel* is included for fun; it also shows you how you can take a well-known fairy tale and update it.

A dramatic play called *The Cat Who Walked by Himself* is included in this chapter, too. This scene gives you a chance to practice your animal characters.

Finally, a scene from *Macbeth* gives you a chance to practice speaking in verse and acting wicked.

Whether you're performing a monologue, a two-character scene, or a ten-character scene, read the entire play to learn about your character and how the scene fits into the entire story.

Whatever script you choose, the activities in the previous chapters will help you prepare your voice and body, focus on the play, define your character, act successfully with the other performers, create costumes and apply makeup that helps set the mood, and create the scenery to give the play a location and time.

Rip van Winkle

A Monologue

This adaptation was originally created by Emanon Theater Company.

Actors often perform monologues for the director when they audition for a play. Here is a monologue performed by a character named Jane (it could just as easily be performed by a boy, too).

★ Character: Jane, age 10
★ Setting: A forest on a mountain side

Jane has gone in search of clues to explain the disappearance of her great, great, great Uncle Rip van Winkle.

JANE:

I'm on a great misadventure today. I'm solving the mystery of the disappearance of my great, great, great Uncle Rip van Winkle. He disappeared hundreds of years ago, and nobody ever found out what happened to him. They say he went up this mountain and never returned, so I'm up here looking for clues. It's very mysterious here in the forest, but I'm not afraid, even though forests can be very scary, like in the story of Snow White. She got lost in a forest, but luckily she found dwarves, so I'm not afraid. Then there was Little Red Riding Hood. She found a wolf, but she got out all right. Hansel and Gretel got lost in a forest, and they found a witch. Oh boy, I guess I am a little afraid. But that's all right, because I'm a brave detective. (*A loud sound is heard offstage.*) What was that? (*Loud sound is heard again; Jane screams and exits in fear.*) I'm getting out of here!

The scene ends.

Other monologues for young people can be found in the following scripts and books in your library:

★ *You're a Good Man, Charlie Brown* by Clark Gesner
★ *Member of the Wedding* by Carson McCullers
★ *Our Town* by Thornton Wilder
★ *Spoon River Anthology* by Charles Aidman
★ *Humorous Monologues* by Martha Bolton
★ *Winning Monologues for Young Actors* by Peg Kehret

The Snow Queen

This monologue is from The Snow Queen. *It was originally adapted by Emanon Theater Company.*

The goblin in this monologue can be played by a male or female actor. This scene requires a few props.

CHARACTER

★ Goblin

GOBLIN:

Oh, that Snow Queen! She really burns me up! What can I do to get her? I know! There must be something I can use in my evil box! Let's see, where did I put my evil box? Have you seen my evil box? *(Looks around.)* Is it here? No. Here? No. Aha! I remember! I hid my evil box under my evil bed! *(Goes offstage to get the evil box.)* Here it is. Now let's see what's in it. *(Pulls out a stuffed animal from the evil box.)* Here's a monster I could sic on her! No, it's too small. *(Pulls out a puppet from the evil box.)* Ah, here's a scary puppet. I could have it chew her up! No, it doesn't have real teeth. *(Pulls out a handful of powder.)* Ah, magic sneezing powder. I could spread it all over her and . . . and . . . and . . . and . . . achoo! *(Sneezes powder away.)* Darn, lost it! Oh, I've got it! My evil mirror! *(Pulls out a mirror.)* This is a magic mirror. I know. You've probably heard of a magic mirror before. There was a magic mirror in *Snow White and the Seven Dwarfs.* Let me see if I can remember the magic words to say to the magic mirror. Mirror, mirror, on the wall, who's the fairest of them all? That's right. Well, this isn't the same mirror; it's better. Here are the magic words to say to this mirror: Mirror, mirror, in my hand, show me evil in the land. Now look in the mirror and see evil! Wait a minute. It's not working. I don't see evil, or anger, or sadness, or any of that great stuff. Maybe it's dirty. *(Wipes off the mirror.)* Let's try again. Mirror, mirror, in my hand, show me evil in the land. Now let's see some monsters! It's still not working. Hey, what's this say on the back? Di-rec-tions. "Directions"? I never read the directions. Maybe I should. Let's see, it says, "Take one evil mirror." Got it. "Take one evil hammer." An evil hammer? I think I've got an evil hammer in my evil box! *(Pulls out a hammer.)* "Break the evil mirror with the evil hammer." Oh, but if I break the mirror, I'll get seven years of bad luck! That's OK. I invented bad luck! Now it says, "Scatter pieces of the evil mirror all around. When a piece lands on some-one, it will make them evil." I like that! Now I'll show that Snow Queen!

Alice in Wonderland

A Monologue

This monologue is from **Alice in Wonderland.** *It was originally adapted by Emanon Theater Company.*

For this monologue, it helps to have an actor playing the white rabbit.

CHARACTER

★ Alice

ALICE *(enters with a book)*:

Hello. Do you see what I have? A book! And it's not just any book. It's a picture book! I've got a picture book filled with wonderful, marvelous, beautiful pictures. I love picture books, don't you? I'm going to sit right down here and look at all the brand-new pictures in my brand-new picture book. *(Opens book; realizes there are no pictures.)* What's this? There are no pictures! How could there be no pictures in my brand-new picture book? This is terrible! *(Calms herself down.)* That's all right; we'll use our imagination. We'll just imagine all the pictures. Like here, for instance—we can imagine a picture of a little stream, and a tree, and a little bunny comes hopping out from behind the tree. *(White Rabbit runs by.)* Did you hear something? It must have been the wind. Now, back to our picture. A little bunny hops along and stops to smell the flowers. *(White Rabbit enters, looks at his watch, gasps, and leaves.)* Did you make that noise? I didn't make that noise. What could have made that noise? A bunny? Oh, I love little bunnies! Maybe I can find it. Here, bunny, bunny, bunny! Here, bunny, bunny, bunny! *(White Rabbit enters. Alice sees how big he is; she gasps; he gasps and runs off.)* Did you see that? That was a big bunny! That was the biggest bunny I've ever seen! No, it couldn't have been. It was just my imagination, once again, running away with me. I'll just go back to reading my book.

WHITE RABBIT *(from offstage)*:

I'm late!

ALICE:

Did you say that? I didn't say that. Who could've said that?

WHITE RABBIT *(from offstage)*:

I'm horribly, horribly tardy!

ALICE:

The rabbit? But rabbits can't talk! That must be one extraordinary rabbit. How curious! I've got to follow that talking rabbit. *(She exits.)*

The scene ends.

The Tale of Jeremy Fisher

A Play

From an adaptation by Emanon Theater Company.

This scene features a storyteller and sound effects. This play has six characters, but if there are only four actors, one actor can play the water beetle and Dr. Turtle and one actor can play the large-mouth bass and Sir Isaac Newton.

CHARACTER

★ Narrator (storyteller)
★ Jeremy Fisher
★ Water Beetle
★ Large-Mouth Bass
★ Dr. Turtle
★ Sir Isaac Newton

NARRATOR:

Once there was a gentleman frog named Jeremy Fisher who decided to have a dinner party, so he invited his friends Sir Isaac Newton and Dr. Turtle. He needed to serve fish at this party, so he had to go fishing. He gathered his fishing pole and tackle box and put on his galoshes.

JEREMY:

Galosh, galosh.

NARRATOR:

And his mackintosh.

JEREMY:

My raincoat.

NARRATOR:

And Jeremy went down to the pond. It was very relaxing, and Jeremy could hear all of the sounds from the pond. Frogs, birds, water . . . *(Pond sound effects are heard.)* After a while, it was time for lunch. Jeremy made himself a butterfly sandwich.

JEREMY:

First, take out two slices of bread. Next, butter the bread. Then find a fly, catch it, put it between the bread, and there you have it—a butterfly sandwich. Yum.

NARRATOR:

Jeremy finished lunch.

JEREMY:

Gulp!

NARRATOR:

When, all of the sudden, a nasty water beetle appeared.

BEETLE *(chanting)*:

Galoshes, galoshes, I like to eat galoshes. Galoshes, galoshes, I like to eat galoshes.

NARRATOR:

And the nasty water beetle stole Jeremy's galoshes!

JEREMY:

I'm galoshless!

NARRATOR:

Well, Jeremy was pretty upset about his galoshes, and just when he thought it was safe, a giant large-mouth bass appeared and saw Jeremy's fishing bobber.

BASS:

I spy a bobber.

NARRATOR:

In one gulp, the large-mouth bass swallowed Jeremy Fisher!

BASS:

I've got a frog in my throat!

NARRATOR:

But just as quickly as he swallowed him, he spit him back out.

BASS:

Yuck! A mackintosh!

NARRATOR:

The large-mouth bass hated the taste of mackintoshes. Jeremy wiped the squishy fish guts off and went home without anything for dinner. When Jeremy's friends arrived that evening . . .

TURTLE:

Jeremy, it's great to see you!

JEREMY:

Hello, Dr. Turtle.

NEWTON:

What smells in here?

JEREMY:

Hello, Newton. I'm afraid I had some bad luck at the pond today, and I have no fish to serve you.

NEWTON AND TURTLE:

No fish?

JEREMY:

But I do have something even better! Butterfly sandwiches. Take your bread, butter it, find a fly, catch it, put it between the bread, and there you have it. *(Newton and Turtle make sandwiches.)*

NARRATOR:

And they had a fine feast. The end.

The North Wind and the Sun

A Play

This is one of Aesop's Fables *that was adapted by Emanon Theater Company.*

CHARACTER

★ Narrator
★ Traveler
★ Kitten
★ North Wind
★ Sun

Traveler and Kitten are onstage. Traveler is wearing a coat.

NARRATOR:

Once upon a time, there was a traveler walking down the road with her kitten. The North Wind *(North Wind enters)* saw the traveler with her coat on tight and bet the sun *(Sun enters)* that he could make the traveler take off her coat before the sun could.

NORTH WIND:

I bet you I can make her take her coat off.

SUN:

Oh, yeah?

NORTH WIND:

Yeah.

SUN:

Oh, yeah?

NORTH WIND:

Yeah!

SUN:

Well, I bet you *I* can make her take her coat off.

NORTH WIND:

Oh, yeah?

SUN:

Yeah.

NORTH WIND:

Oh, yeah?

SUN:

Yeah!

NORTH WIND:

How much you want to bet?

SUN:

A nickel.

Aesop, the author of *Aesop's Fables*, was a Roman slave who wrote stories from prison.

NORTH WIND:

You're on. *(They shake hands.)*

NARRATOR:

The north wind went first. He took a deep breath and blew as hard as he could. *(North Wind blows.)*

TRAVELER:

It's a little chilly here.

KITTEN:

Meow. Chilly. Meow.

NARRATOR:

But it wasn't quite enough. So he tried again and blew even harder. *(North Wind blows.)*

TRAVELER AND KITTEN *(getting blown around)*:

Whoa! Whoa!

NARRATOR:

But the traveler pulled her coat on tighter.

TRAVELER:

It's so cold.

KITTEN:

Meow. Cold. Meow.

NARRATOR:

Next, it was the sun's turn. The sun came out and beamed down upon the traveler. She shone as bright and happy as she possibly could. *(Sun shines on traveler.)*

TRAVELER:

Oh, the sun's out. It's getting warmer.

KITTEN:

Meow. Nice. Meow.

NARRATOR:

But it wasn't quite enough, so she tried again, and shown even brighter. *(Sun shines bright.)*

TRAVELER:

It's really hot out.

KITTEN:

Meow. Hot. Meow.

TRAVELER:

It's so hot I don't need this coat anymore. *(Traveler takes off her coat.)*

SUN:

I win! I win!

NORTH WIND:

I guess it's better to be warm and kind than cold and fierce.

NARRATOR:

The end.

The Importance of Being Earnest

A Scene

You can find a copy of The Importance of Being Earnest *by Oscar Wilde at your library. This scene has been simplified from the original version.*

In this scene, it's important to know that both Cecily and Gwendoline think they are engaged to be married to Ernest. The two men they are actually engaged to are named Jack and Algernon, but both men lied about their names. In this scene, Gwendoline meets Cecily, who she believes to be her fiancé's ward, which is an adopted child, or someone he looks after. When she finds out Cecily is engaged to Ernest, she mistakenly assumes they are engaged to the same man. The scene becomes very funny, as they hurl insults at each other while maintaining their proper manners. (British comedy is full of humor based on misunderstandings like this one.)

CHARACTERS

★ Gwendoline
★ Cecily

SETTING

★ Cecily's garden

CECILY:

Allow me to introduce myself to you. My name is Cecily Cardew.

GWENDOLINE:

Cecily Cardew? What a very sweet name! Something tells me we are going to be great friends. I like you already more than I can say. My first impressions of people are never wrong.

CECILY:

How nice of you to like me so much after we have known each other for such a short time. Do sit down.

GWENDOLINE:

Do you mind my looking at you through my glasses?

CECILY:

Oh! Not at all, Gwendoline. I am very fond of being looked at.

GWENDOLINE:

You are here on a short visit, I suppose.

CECILY:

Oh, no! I live here.

GWENDOLINE:

Really?

CECILY:

Yes. I am Mr. Worthing's ward.

GWENDOLINE:

Oh! It is strange he never mentioned to me that he had a ward. How secretive of him! He grows more interesting hourly. I am not sure, however, that the news delights me. I am very fond of you, Cecily; I have liked you ever since I met you! But now that I know you are Mr. Worthing's ward, I wish that you were, well, just a little older than you appear to be, and not quite so very alluring in appearance. Ernest has a strong upright nature but . . .

CECILY:

I beg your pardon, Gwendoline—did you say Ernest?

GWENDOLINE:

Yes.

CECILY:

Oh, but it is not Mr. Ernest Worthing who is my guardian. It is his brother.

GWENDOLINE:

Ernest never mentioned to me that he had a brother.

CECILY:

I am sorry to say they have not been on good terms for a long time.

GWENDOLINE:

Ah, that accounts for it. Of course you are quite sure that it is not Mr. Ernest Worthing who is your guardian?

CECILY:

Quite sure. In fact, I am going to be his.

GWENDOLINE:

I beg your pardon?

CECILY:

Dearest Gwendoline, there is no reason why I should keep it a secret. Mr. Ernest Worthing and I are engaged to be married.

GWENDOLINE:

My darling Cecily, I think there must be some slight error. Mr. Ernest Worthing is engaged to me.

CECILY:

Ernest proposed to me exactly ten minutes ago.

GWENDOLYN:

He asked me to be his wife yesterday afternoon at 5:30. I am so sorry, dear Cecily, but I am afraid I have the prior claim.

CECILY:

I feel bound to point out that since Ernest proposed to you he clearly has changed his mind.

GWENDOLINE (*looking around*):

Quite a well kept garden, Miss Cardew.

CECILY:

So glad you like it, Miss Fairfax.

GWENDOLINE:

I had no idea there were any flowers in the country.

CECILY:

Oh, flowers are as common here, Miss Fairfax, as people are in London.

GWENDOLINE:

Personally I cannot understand how anybody manages to exist in the country, if anybody who is anybody does. The country always bores me to death.

CECILY:

May I offer you some tea, Miss Fairfax?

GWENDOLINE:

Thank you. (*Aside to audience*) Detestable girl! But I require tea!

CECILY:

Sugar?

GWENDOLINE:

No, thank you. (*Cecily puts four lumps of sugar into Gwendoline's cup.*)

CECILY:

Cake or bread and butter?

GWENDOLINE:

Bread and butter, please. (*Cecily cuts a very large slice of cake and puts it on the tray. Gwendoline takes a sip of the tea and notices the cake.*) You have filled my tea with lumps of sugar, and though I asked for bread and butter, you have given me cake. I warn you, Miss Cardew, you may go too far.

CECILY:

To save my poor, innocent, trusting boy from any other girl, there are no lengths to which I would not go.

GWENDOLINE:

From the moment I saw you I distrusted you. My first impressions of people are always right.

CECILY:

It seems to me, Miss Fairfax, that I am wasting your valuable time. No doubt you have other visits of a similar character to make in the neighborhood.*

The scene ends.

---

* This humorous insult suggests that Gwendoline goes door to door claiming to be engaged to other women's fiancés.

Rapunzel

A Scene

From an adaptation by Emanon Theater Company.

This is a fun play that gives your audience a role.

CHARACTERS

★ Witch
★ Father
★ Mother
★ Demon Radish
★ Ogre

SCENE 1:

Stage left is the house of Mother and Father; stage right is the witch's garden.

The witch enters.

WITCH:

Hello!

FATHER, MOTHER, AND AUDIENCE:

Hello!

WITCH:

Hello!

FATHER, MOTHER, AND AUDIENCE:

Hello!

WITCH:

I'm a witch. I can do magic. *(Pulls out flowers.)* I can cast spells. *(To Father)* Cluck like a chicken!

FATHER:

Cluck, cluck.

WITCH:

I can do all kinds of wonderful, horrible things, but mostly I spend my time tending to my lovely garden. Lately, I have been wishing that I had a child to keep me company. How could I get a child? It just occurred to me—are any of you children? Perhaps I could take you home with me. No, I really want a little baby. There's a happy little neighbor couple next door. They're going to have a baby. Perhaps I could borrow their child for a few years. What I need to do is make them want something of mine so that they'll trade with me.

(rapping) *I'm a witch, I'm a witch,*
And I really want a kid,
So I must convince my neighbors
They don't want one, never did!
I could give the wife a craving

That will make her ache and pine
For something from my garden
Till she makes her child mine!
I'm a witch, I'm a witch,
So I'm gonna work a charm.
Gonna go into my garden
To my little witch farm.
Gonna grow me a radish,
Grow it big, grow it wild.
Gonna grow a demon radish
To steal that child!

DEMON RADISH *(rapping)*:

I'm awake. I'm alive,
And I'm big, and I'm wild.
Gonna be your demon radish
Gonna go steal you a child.
I'm awake, I'm alive,
Just you wait and see.
Gonna make your pregnant neighbor
Hungry for me.

OGRE:

Hello. My name is Grumble Bonecruncher, but you can call me Ogre. I'm seven, and when you're an ogre and you're seven, your dad says, "Get out!" So now I live over there. I'm out looking for some friends. It's real hard to meet folks when your name's Bonecruncher. People think I just want to crunch their bones, but I think I can help people. It's just that I'm not so much a people person. Well, wish me luck.

MOTHER, FATHER, AND AUDIENCE:

Good luck!

MOTHER:

Oh, I'm so happy. We're having a balloon.

FATHER:

A balloon? Are we having a party?

MOTHER:

Oh, no. I meant to say, "We're having a beanbag."

FATHER:

A beanbag? What are we having a beanbag for?

MOTHER:

Oh, dear. *(To audience)* What are we having?

AUDIENCE:

A baby!

MOTHER:

Oh, yes, that's right. We're having a baby.

FATHER:

Yes, a baby. I'm so happy we're finally having a baby.

MOTHER:

What are you baking there?

FATHER:

I'm baking a pie.

MOTHER:

What kind of pie?

FATHER:

An apple pie.

MOTHER:

Oh, that sounds real good, but I'm not sure that's exactly what I'm craving.

DEMON RADISH:

You are craving a radish.

FATHER:

Well, what kind of pie would you like?

DEMON RADISH:

Radish.

MOTHER:

How about a raspberry pie?

DEMON RADISH:

You want a radish.

FATHER:

That sounds good. I'll bake you a raspberry pie.

DEMON RADISH:

Radish.

MOTHER:

No, that's not what I want. I want a—

DEMON RADISH:

Radish.

MOTHER:

Rhubarb. Yes, a rhubarb.

DEMON RADISH:

Radish.

FATHER:

You never liked rhubarb before.

DEMON RADISH:

Radish.

MOTHER:

I know, but I must have some . . . *(to audience)* What do I want?

DEMON RADISH AND AUDIENCE:

Radish!

MOTHER:

Radish! That's what it is. I must have a radish.

FATHER:

A radish? Where am I supposed to get a radish?

DEMON RADISH:

In the witch's garden.

MOTHER:

In the wombat's garden.

FATHER:

Huh?

DEMON RADISH:

Witch's garden.

MOTHER:

In the worm's garden.

FATHER:

Where?

DEMON RADISH:

Witch's garden.

MOTHER:

In the witch's garden!

FATHER:

The witch's garden? I can't go in there!

MOTHER:

Oh, but you must. I must have a radish from the witch's garden. Go, please.

FATHER:

If I must, I shall. *(To audience)* What do you think? Should I go steal a radish from the witch's garden?

AUDIENCE:

No!

FATHER:

No? OK. *(To Mother)* The audience says I shouldn't steal from the witch's garden.

MOTHER:

But I need those radishes now! *(To audience)* Don't worry. He'll be fine.

FATHER:

What's the worst that could happen? *(Goes into the garden. Ogre knocks on the door.)*

MOTHER:

Come in.

OGRE:

My name's Grumble Bonecruncher, but you can call me Ogre. Do you have a cup of tuna I could borrow?

MOTHER:

Ogre? Oh, dear. No, I'm sorry; you'll have to go.

FATHER *(to audience)*:

Do you see the witch?

AUDIENCE:

No.

FATHER:

Shhh! Be very quiet. If she catches me, she'll put some kind of strange spell on me, so be very, very quiet. *(Trips on a garbage-can lid.)* Shhh! I said be quiet. Now, where's a radish? I don't see any radishes. *(Witch and Demon Radish throw radishes at Father. Demon Radish knocks him over. Father takes radishes. Witch laughs.)* I've got to get out of here! *(Runs back to Mother.)* Here.

MOTHER:

Thank you. These radishes are delicious.

FATHER:

You don't know what I went through to get these.

DEMON RADISH:

You need more radishes.

MOTHER:

Oh, these are the best things I've ever tasted.

DEMON RADISH:

Radish.

MOTHER:

I must have more radishes.

FATHER:

More radishes?

DEMON RADISH:

Or else you will perish.

MOTHER:

If I don't get more radishes, I'll pop!

FATHER:

Pop?

DEMON RADISH:

Perish.

MOTHER:

No, I mean, I'll pollinate.

FATHER:

Huh?

DEMON RADISH:

Perish.

MOTHER:

If I don't get more radishes, I'll—

DEMON RADISH:

Perish.

MOTHER:

Perish! Yes, I'll perish! You must get me more radishes! *(Ogre knocks on the door.)*

FATHER:

Come in.

OGRE:

Hello, my name's Grumble Bonecruncher, but you can call me Ogre.

FATHER:

Hello, Ogre.

MOTHER:

I'm going to die without radishes!

OGRE:

I'm new around here.

FATHER:

Oh, welcome to the neighborhood.

MOTHER:

Help me!

OGRE:

Thanks. So, what do you do?

FATHER:

I'm a baker.

MOTHER:

Help me now!

OGRE:

A baker? That's great. Ever bake tuna pies?

FATHER:

No, mostly apple, cherry, and blueberry.

MOTHER:

I must have a radish now!

OGRE:

Oh, those are OK, but I really like fish.

MOTHER:

I'm going to die if you don't get me a radish now!

FATHER:

You know, I think I'd better help my wife here. Perhaps we could talk later.

OGRE:

That would be great. See you.

FATHER *(to Mother)*:

I'm going. I'm going to get you some more radishes. I'll be right back. *(Sneaks into garden.)* Shhh. Be very quiet, I don't want to bother the witch. *(Demon Radish throws radishes at him. Father picks them up, turns around, and runs into Witch.)*

WITCH:

Hello.

FATHER *(startled)*:

Oh, uh, hi.

WITCH:

Come over for a little visit with your neighbor?

FATHER:

Oh, no, I was, uh, just on my way to the market.

WITCH:

To sell my radishes?

FATHER:

What radishes? Oh, these radishes? How did they get there? I must have been sleepwalking. I didn't realize—

WITCH:

Oh, really?

FATHER:

Yes, uh, I mean, no. I mean, I was just passing through and these radishes jumped up at me. I almost tripped. You know, you could get sued.

WITCH:

You were stealing my radishes.

FATHER:

Stealing? Me? No, it's just that—

MOTHER:

Help! I'm dying!

FATHER:

You see, my wife is pregnant, and she says she will die without radishes.

WITCH:

If what you say is true, you may have all you need.

FATHER:

Oh, thank you. You're kind.

WITCH:

But you must give me something in return.

MOTHER:

I must have radishes!

FATHER:

Sure, would you like a pie?

WITCH:

No, I don't need any pies.

FATHER:

Well, what do you want?

WITCH:

Let's see. *(To audience)* What do I want?

MOTHER:

It's the big one!

FATHER:

Anything! You can have anything! I must get these to my wife right away. *(Grabs radishes and goes to wife.)*

WITCH:

Now's my chance.

FATHER *(to Mother)*:

Here you are.

MOTHER.

Oh, thank you.

FATHER:

I'm going to finish baking these pies. *(Witch knocks on the door.)*

MOTHER:

Come in.

WITCH:

I gave your husband some radishes from my garden

MOTHER:

Thank you. They were delicious.

WITCH:

Yes, well, he promised me that I could have something in return.

MOTHER:

Oh, sure. You betcha.

DEMON RADISH:

Give her your child.

MOTHER:

You can have our child.

WITCH:

Thank you.

WITCH AND DEMON RADISH:

We got the child! We got the child!

DEMON RADISH:

We got him!

WITCH:

Her! It's going to be a girl.

FATHER:

Who was that?

MOTHER:

Oh, that was the witch. I told her she could have our chicken.

FATHER:

Phew. I though you said something else.

MOTHER:

No, not chicken—I told her she could have our chia pet.

FATHER:

You're sure? You're quite sure you didn't say "child"?

MOTHER:

Well, I'm not exactly sure.

FATHER:

Ogre, you were here. What did she say?

MOTHER:

What did I say?

FATHER:

What did she say?

OGRE *(struggling)*:

She said "child."

FATHER:

Oh, no!

MOTHER:

I was sabotaged by a demon radish!

OGRE:

That'll happen.

FATHER:

That's all right. We'll think of a way to stop her.

OGRE:

I could help!

MOTHER:

How do you stop a witch?

OGRE:

We could drop a house on her. I hear that works on witches.

FATHER:

Great idea.

MOTHER:

Even Ogre isn't big enough to lift a house.

FATHER:

Right.

MOTHER:

We could push her into an oven. I heard of two children who did that to a witch once.

FATHER:

But I've got pies in the oven.

OGRE:

She's got a bun in the oven.

MOTHER:

Oh, yes.

FATHER:

Let's melt her with water.

OGRE:

Good idea.

MOTHER:

Take your squirt gun.

OGRE:

I'll distract her while you squirt her.

FATHER:

It's worth a try.

OGRE *(crossing to Witch)*:

A singing telegram for the witch.

WITCH:

> A singing telegram for me? (*Ogre does song and dance while Father squirts Witch.*) Water? You fool! That only works in the movies! In real life it does nothing to me— it makes my demon radish grow even bigger! (*Father, Mother, and Ogre exit.*)

WITCH (*to audience*)**:**

> There's nothing they can do. A deal is a deal. All I have to do is wait for it to be born, and the child will be mine!

The scene ends.

The Cat Who Walked by Himself

A Play

This scene is an adaptation of a story by Rudyard Kipling.

This scene is written in the style of story theater, incorporating narration with dialogue. This play gives you a chance to use your animal costumes.

CHARACTERS

★ Cat
★ Dog
★ Horse
★ Cow
★ Sheep
★ Pig
★ Man
★ Woman

CAT:

Hear and listen, for this story happened when the tame animals were wild.

DOG:

The dog was wild.

HORSE:

The horse was wild.

COW:

The cow was wild.

SHEEP:

The sheep was wild.

PIG:

The pig was wild.

DOG:

And they walked in the wild woods.

CAT:

But the wildest of all was the cat. He walked by himself.

MAN:

Of course the man was wild, too. He was dreadfully wild. He didn't even begin to become tame until he met the woman.

WOMAN *(to Man)*:

I do not like living in your wild ways. I will pick out a cave, lay clean sand on the floor, light a nice fire at the back of the cave, and hang a dried wild-horse skin across the opening of the cave. Wipe your feet, dear, when you come in. Now we'll keep house.

MAN:

That night, they ate a great meal. Then Man went to sleep in front of the fire.

WOMAN:

But Woman stayed up combing her hair. *(To Man)* Look at this bone of mutton from dinner; see the wonderful marks on it. *(To audience)* Woman began to sing. She made the first singing magic in the world.

CAT:

Out in the wild woods, all the wild animals gathered around to see the light of the fire and hear the singing.

HORSE:

Why have Man and Woman made that great light in the cave?

DOG:

I will go and see. *(To Cat)* Cat, come with me.

CAT:

Nenni! I am the cat who walks by himself. I will not come.

DOG:

Then we can never be friends again. *(To audience)* Wild Dog went to the cave.

CAT:

All places are alike to me. Why should I not go, too, and see and come away at my own liking? *(To audience)* So Cat slipped away to the cave and hid himself where he could hear.

DOG:

When Wild Dog reached the cave, he sniffed the beautiful smell of roast mutton.

WOMAN:

Here comes the first wild thing out of the wild woods. What do you want?

DOG:

What is this that smells so good?

WOMAN:

Taste and try.

DOG:

Wild Dog gnawed the bone. *(To Woman)* This is more delicious than anything I have ever tasted. Give me another.

WOMAN:

Wild thing out of the wild woods, help us to hunt through the day and guard this cave at night, and I will give you as many roast bones as you need.

CAT:

Ah, this is a very wise woman, but she is not so wise as I am.

DOG:

I will help you hunt through the day, and at night I will guard your cave.

CAT:

Ah, that is a very foolish dog.

MAN:

Man woke up. *(To Woman)* What is Wild Dog doing here?

WOMAN:

His name is not Wild Dog anymore—it is First Friend, because he will be our friend for always and always.

We can take him with us when we go hunting. *(To audience)* The next night the woman looked at the shoulder of mutton bone and found a big, broad bone from the blade. She made the second singing magic.

HORSE:

I wonder what has happened to Wild Dog. I will go and see why Wild Dog has not returned. *(To Cat)* Cat, come with me.

CAT:

Nenni. I am the cat who walks by himself. I will not come.

HORSE:

Very well.

CAT *(to audience)*:

But Cat followed softly.

WOMAN:

Here comes the second wild thing out of the wild woods. What do you want?

HORSE:

Where is Wild Dog?

WOMAN:

You did not come here for Wild Dog but for this good grass.

HORSE:

That is true. Give it to me to eat.

WOMAN:

Wild thing out of the wild woods, bend your wild head and wear what I give you, and you shall eat the wonderful grass three times a day.

CAT:

Ah, this is a clever woman, but she is not so clever as I am.

HORSE:

I will be your servant for the sake of the wonderful grass.

CAT:

Ah, that is a very foolish horse.

MAN:

Man came home with Dog. *(To Woman)* What is Wild Horse doing here?

WOMAN:

His name is not Wild Horse anymore but First Servant. He will carry us from place to place for always and always. We can ride on his back when we go hunting.

COW:

The next day, Wild Cow came up to the cave.

CAT:

And everything happened just the same as before.

COW:

I promise to give you milk every day in exchange for the wonderful grass.

MAN:

Man came home with Dog and Horse. *(To Woman)* What is Wild Cow doing here?

WOMAN:

Her name is not Wild Cow anymore but the Giver of Good Food. She will give us warm, white milk for always and always.

CAT:

I wonder who will be next.

SHEEP:

Not I.

PIG:

Not I.

CAT:

I shall go there myself and see. *(To Woman)* Where did Wild Cow go?

WOMAN:

Go back to the woods again, for I have put away the magic blade bone, and we have no more need for friends or servants.

CAT:

I am not a friend nor a servant. I am the cat who walks by himself. I wish to come into your cave.

WOMAN:

Then why didn't you come with Dog on the first night?

CAT:

Has Dog told tales of me?

WOMAN:

You are the cat who walks by himself. You are neither friend nor servant. Go away and walk by yourself.

CAT:

Must I never come into the cave? Must I never sit by the fire? Must I never drink the warm, white milk? You are very wise and very beautiful. You should not be cruel to a cat.

WOMAN:

I knew I was wise, but I did not know I was beautiful. I will make a bargain with you. If ever I say one word in your praise, you may come into the cave.

CAT:

And if you say two words in my praise?

WOMAN:

I never shall, but if I do, you may drink the warm, white milk three times a day for always and always.

CAT:

Don't forget our bargain. *(To audience)* The cat went far away and hid himself until Sheep and Pig came.

SHEEP:

There is a baby in the cave.

PIG:

He is new and pink and fat and small. Man and Woman are very fond of him.

CAT:

Ah, but what is the baby fond of?

SHEEP:

He is fond of all things that are soft and that tickle.

PIG:

He is fond of warm things to hold in his arms when he goes to sleep.

SHEEP:

He is fond of being played with.

CAT:

Ah, then my time has come.

The scene ends.

Macbeth

A Scene

In this scene from *Macbeth*, by William Shakespeare, three witches are making a magic brew so that they can see into the future.

CHARACTERS

★ Witch 1
★ Witch 2
★ Witch 3

WITCH 1:
> Thrice the brinded cat hath mew'd.

WITCH 2:
> Thrice and once the hedge-pig whin'd.

WITCH 3:
> Harper cries: 'Tis time, 'tis time.

WITCH 1:
> Round about the cauldron go;
> In the poison'd entrails throw.
> Toad, that under coldest stone
> Days and nights has thirty-one
> Swelter'd venom, sleeping got,
> Boil thou first i' the charmed pot.

ALL:
> Double, double, toil and trouble:
> Fire burn; and, cauldron bubble.

WITCH 2:
> Fillet of a fenny snake,
> In the cauldron boil and bake;
> Eye of newt, and toe of frog,
> Wool of bat, and tongue of dog,
> Adder's fork, and blind-worm's sting,
> Lizard's leg, and howlet's wing,
> For a charm of powerful trouble,
> Like a hell-broth boil and bubble.

ALL:
> Double, double, toil and trouble:
> Fire, burn; and, cauldron, bubble.

WITCH 3:
> Scale of dragon, tooth of wolf;
> Witches' mummy; maw, and gulf,
> Of the ravin'd salt-sea shark;
> Root of hemlock, digg'd i' the dark;
> Liver of blaspheming Jew;
> Gall of goat, and slips of yew,

Sliver'd in the moon's eclipse;
Nose of Turk, and Tartar's lips;
Ditch-deliver'd by a drab,
Make the gruel thick and slab:
Add thereto a tiger's chaudron,
For the ingredients of our cauldron.

ALL:

Double, double, toil and trouble:
Fire, burn; and, cauldron, bubble.

WITCH 2:

Cool it with a baboon's blood;
Then the charm is firm and good.

The scene ends.

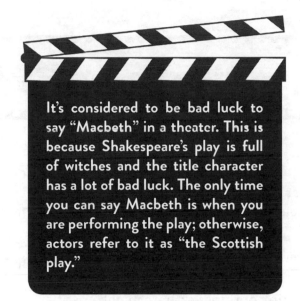

It's considered to be bad luck to say "Macbeth" in a theater. This is because Shakespeare's play is full of witches and the title character has a lot of bad luck. The only time you can say Macbeth is when you are performing the play; otherwise, actors refer to it as "the Scottish play."

Pirate with One

The scenario is that a pirate is dying. When asked who killed him, the pirate says, with his last words, that it was a pirate who only had one. . . . Then he dies without finishing the sentence. The Captain questions a series of pirates who have only one of something, trying to solve the mystery.

Below is a version of the sketch written at Play On Drama Camp, but you can write your own. Think of things a pirate might have only one of; then think of a funny name for the pirate; finally, think of an alibi for him.

(Pirate Billy Bob Joe is dying.)

CAPTAIN:
Pirate Billy Bob Joe! Who did this to you?

BBJ:
It was pirate with only one . . . *(He dies.)*

CAPTAIN:
One what? No matter, I'll find the scurvy dog who did this dastardly deed. *(Four-Eyes enters.)*

CAPTAIN:
What's your name?

FOUR EYES:
Four Eyes.

CAPTAIN:
You only have one eye, and I'm looking for a pirate with one of something.

FOUR EYES:
I see.

CAPTAIN:
Where were you when Pirate Billy Bob Joe was murdered?

FOUR EYES:

I was whale watching.

CAPTAIN:

Whale watching, eh? That's fishy.

FOUR EYES:

Not really. They're mammals, you know.

CAPTAIN:

True. You're free to go. *(Four Eyes exits; Peg Leg enters.)*

CAPTAIN:

What's your name?

PEG:

Peg.

CAPTAIN:

Peg what?

PEG:

Peg Leg.

CAPTAIN:

I see you have only one leg, and I'm looking for a pirate with one of something, so where were you when Billy Bob Joe was murdered?

PEG:

I was in a three-legged race.

CAPTAIN:

A three-legged race?

PEG:

Yes, with my brother, Pant Leg.

CAPTAIN:

All right. You're free to go. *(Peg Leg exits; Pop U. Lar enters.)*

CAPTAIN:

What's your name?

POP:

Pop U. Lar.

CAPTAIN:

Mr. Pop U. Lar, I am looking for a pirate with only one of something. What do you have only one of?

POP:

Friends.

CAPTAIN:

You only have one friend?

POP.

Yes.

CAPTAIN:

Where were you when Billy Bob Joe was killed?

POP:

I was at a cat party.

CAPTAIN:

How sad. You're free to go. *(Pop U. Lar exits; Happy enters, laughing.)*

CAPTAIN:

What's your name?

HAPPY:

Happy!

CAPTAIN:

What do you only have one of?

HAPPY:

Emotions! I'm always happy!

CAPTAIN:

I see. Where were you when Billy Bob Joe was murdered.

HAPPY:

At a funeral. *(Laughs.)*

CAPTAIN:

How sad.

HAPPY:

I know. *(Laughs.)* Tragic. *(Laughs.)*

CAPTAIN:

You're free to go. *(Happy exits; Dude enters.)*

CAPTAIN:

What's your name?

DUDE:

Dude.

CAPTAIN:

What do you have only one of, Dude?

DUDE:

I only have dance move. *(He dances.)*

CAPTAIN:

Where were you when Billy Bob Joe was killed?

DUDE:

I was on *Dancing with the Stars*.

CAPTAIN:

With only one dance move?

DUDE:

Yep.

CAPTAIN:

You're free to go . . . for now. *(Dude exits; Einstein enters.)*

CAPTAIN:

What's your name?

EINSTEIN:

Uh, Einstein.

CAPTAIN:

All right, Einstein, what do you only have one of?

EINSTEIN:

Uh, brain cells.

CAPTAIN:

You only have one brain cell?

EINSTEIN:

Uh.

CAPTAIN:

So, where were you when Billy Bob Joe was killed?

EINSTEIN:

I was at a mathlete competition.

CAPTAIN:

You're a mathlete?

EINSTEIN:

No, I just like it when they say "algebra." Get it? Al-ge-*bra*!

CAPTAIN:

I give up! Audience, you choose. By show of applause, is it Four Eyes with his one eye? Peg Leg with her one leg? Pop U. Lar with her one friend? Happy with her one emotion? Dude with his one dance move? Or Einstein with her one brain cell? (*Whichever one the audience selects gets arrested.*)

The scene ends.

Pandora's Box

As the Greek myth of Pandora's box goes, the Gods created Pandora and blessed her with many attributes. They also gave her a box and told her never to open it. Her curiosity overcame her, and she opened the box and released many terrible things into the world. But, in addition to those terrible things, she released hope as well.

This sketch was performed by Code Red Vines, the comedy team from Play On, at the 2011 Chicago Sketch Comedy Festival. However you can create your own version. Write all of the attributes you think the gods should give Pandora. Then write all of the terrible things that she releases from her box. Notice how items are usually grouped in threes, with the third one always being the funniest.

NARRATOR:

Hephaestus made Pandora out of clay and then brought the statue to life.

HEPHAESTUS:

It's alive! It's alive!

NARRATOR:

The gods granted the woman many gifts.

GODDESS OF BEAUTY:

The gift of beauty. As beautiful as Emma Watson.

PANDORA:

Hermione is beautiful.

GODDESS OF CHARM:

The gift of charm . . . like a prince . . . or a frog . . . or a frog prince.

POPCORN GOD:

And the gift of a jumbo buttered popcorn.

GOD OF CUNNING:

The gift of cunning, like Bond . . . James Bond.

GOD OF WIT:

The gift of wit, like Theodore Geisel.

PANDORA:

Who?

GOD OF WIT:

Dr. Seuss.

GOD OF ELOQUENCE:

The gift of eloquence, like a fancy French bathroom with a bidet.

PANDORA:

What's a "bidet"?

GOD OF ELOQUENCE:

It's a butt washer.

GOD OF SKILL:

The gift of skill, like juggling or breakdancing. Hit it! (*Gods all dance for a moment.*)

MUFFIN GOD:

The gift of muffins.

PANDORA:

They're like ugly cupcakes.

MUFFIN GOD:

Yes, but you can pretend they're healthy.

PANDORA:

Ah.

NARRATOR:

Then Zeus gave her a box and told her never to open it. But Pandora always wondered what was in the box.

OTHERS (*whispering*):

Open it. Open it. Open the box.

NARRATOR:

She was very tempted to open the box.

OTHERS:

Open it. Open it. Open the box.

NARRATOR:

Finally, her curiosity overwhelmed her.

OTHERS:

Open the box, girl!

PANDORA (*opening the box*):

Huh—nothing. I knew nothing would happen. (*Hears a clicking sound.*) What's that clicking sound? (*Others enter, clicking pens.*) Oh, no! Clicky pens!

NARRATOR:

Other things came out of the box, such as hate.

HATE:

I hate homework.

NARRATOR:

And anger.

ANGER (*yelling*):

I hate clowns!

NARRATOR:

And price gouging.

POPCORN GOD:

That jumbo popcorn now costs you $8.95, plus tax!

NARRATOR:

Sickness came out.

SICKNESS (*walks by coughing and sneezing*):

I think I have swine flu.

NARRATOR:

And poverty.

POVERTY:

Please, sir, can I have some more?

NARRATOR:

And as-seen-on-TV products.

SALESPERSON:

OxiClean! Perfect Brownie Pan! Snuggie!

NARRATOR:

Sadness came out.

SADNESS (*walks by crying*):

I can't believe Lindsay Lohan ruined her career. It's so sad.

NARRATOR:

And despair.

DESPAIR:

I'm Lindsay Lohan. I need a job.

PANDORA:

How are all of you fitting into this box?

NARRATOR:

Weakness came out.

WEAKNESS:

I can't even lift a cornflake.

NARRATOR:

And fear.

FEAR (*runs by yelling*):

Oh, no! It's Freddy Kruger!

NARRATOR:

And worst of all . . . horrible music.

JUSTIN:

Hi, I'm Justin Bieber. (*Pandora screams.*)

NARRATOR:

The last thing to come out of the box was hope.

HOPE:

And some silly bands. They're colorfully shaped.

NARRATOR:

So, to this day, humans still have hope.

HOPE:

And silly bands. (*All other actors throw silly bands at Pandora.*)

NARRATOR:

The end.

Acknowledgments

Viola Spolin, author of *Improvisation for the Theater, Theater Games for Rehearsal,* and *Theater Games for the Classroom,* first introduced the idea of teaching theater through games. She inspired many of the concepts and originated some of the techniques found in this book. She has been a great inspiration for me and helped to instill a love for theater in me at a very young age. As a child, I played many of her games without realizing where they originated, how important they are in theater, and how much I was learning—I only knew I was having a lot of fun. I hope that others enjoy this book as much as I have enjoyed the books of Viola Spolin.

I'm indebted to the following people and organizations: Stephanie and Joe Albright, Josh Andrews, Arnold Aprill, Martin Bany, Nancy and John Bany, Barat College, Blue Lake Fine Arts Camp, Fran Brumlik, the Cherry family, City Lit Theater, Geoff Coates, Code Red Vines, Columbia College, Diego Colon, Martin de Maat, the Emanon Ensemble, Jack Farrell, Leslie Felbain, Dan Gold, Jayme Gordon, Larry Grimm, Rachel Hadlock, Amy Harmon, Kristie Hassinger, Norm Holly, Ashley Hugen, Illinois Theater Association, Illustrated Theater Company, Improv Playhouse, Hope Kaye, King Lab Drama Club, Sarah Levine, Anne Libera, Susie Lindenbaum, Julie Lockhart, Jason Lubow, Nancy Maes, Laura Maloney, Marionette Playhouse, Terry McCabe, Anthony McKinney, Brad Mott, Susan Osbourne-Mott, Mouth to Mouth, Sheldon Patinkin, Jerry Proffit, Kim Prichard, Laura Pruden, Jason Raymer, Danny Robles, Lisa Rosenthal-Hogarth, Melissa Rubens, Rick Schnier, the Second City, Shanta, Cheryl Sloane, Klahr Thorsen, Janet Tuegel, Tiffany U. Trent, Vernon Hills High School, K. Michelle Williams, Brian Winters, David Woolley, and Wright State University.

217

Glossary of Theatrical Terms

actor: Any theatrical performer; refers to either a male or female performer.

backdrop: A large, painted piece of cloth that is used for scenery in a play.

blackout: When all the lights are simultaneously turned off onstage. A blackout is an effective technique to end a scene.

blocking: Refers to where an actor stands onstage and how the actor moves onstage.

calling the show: Telling the light and sound-board operators when to fade or bring up the lights and sound throughout a performance.

cast: A group of actors in a play.

casting: Assigning parts and duties to actors.

casting call: An audition for a show in which actors try out for and are cast in each character role.

center stage: The middle of the stage.

choreographer: The person who designs and teaches all of the dances in a theatrical production; the person who works with the musical director and the director to make certain the dance movements work well with other production elements.

costume designer: The person who creates what actors wear in a performance.

creative drama: Using dramatic skills and tools, such as pantomime, puppets, and masks, to create stories, scenes, characters, and plays.

cross: "Cross" is used in place of the word "walk." For instance, a director will say, "Cross to stage right."

curtain call: The time at the end of a play when an actor receives applause from the audience for her performance.

director: The person who casts a play and is in charge of an actor's movement onstage.

downstage: The area of the stage that is closest to the audience.

ensemble: A group of people who work together for a common purpose.

enunciating: Pronouncing or clearly saying every syllable and consonant.

flat: A flat piece of scenery.

follow-spot operator: The person who shines a spot light on the actor who is speaking during a play.

giving focus: When an actor does not move or speak in order to give attention to another actor who is moving or speaking.

good stage picture: When the audience can clearly see everyone onstage during a play.

house: Where the audience sits in a theater.

improvisation (*also known as* improv): A drama that is created on the spur of the moment, without any advance preparation; that is, making it up as you go along.

in character: When an actor behaves or speaks in a way a specific character would.

isolate: To move a specific part of your body while keeping the rest of your body still.

isolation: Warming up and concentrating on one part of the body at a time; an exercise that helps actors prepare their bodies to move freely.

light-board operator: A person who fades the lights up and down for a stage play.

light booth: A place in a theater where the light and sound boards are located.

lighting designer: The person who creates the lighting plan for a play that simulates the time of day and location for every scene's action.

makeup designer: The person who makes an actor's face resemble the character he is portraying in a theatrical performance.

mime: An actor who performs without speaking.

monologue: A scene for one actor who is speaking aloud to herself, to another character, or to the audience.

musical director: The person who works with the director and choreographer to see that the music in a play fits in with the acting and the dancing; he directs the actors in the music for the play and is in charge of the musicians.

object transformation: When an actor becomes an object.

offstage: A part of the stage that is not visible to the audience.

onstage: A part of the stage visible to the audience.

pantomime: A performance in which the actors do not speak.

plot: The events in a story.

producer: A person who supervises or finances the production of a stage or screen production or a radio or television program.

production meeting: A meeting where designers and directors meet to discuss the backstage elements of a play.

projection: To speak loudly.

prop: Any object used by an actor in a scene.

props master: The person in charge of getting or making any items carried onstage by actors; sometimes called a "properties" or "props" designer.

proscenium stage: A stage where the audience is on only one side.

set: The scenery or background for a play.

set designer: The person who creates the scenery—the background or setting for a play.

sound-board operator: The person who operates the music and/or sound effects for a play.

sound designer: The person who is in charge of recording all sound effects or recorded music that will be needed during a play.

stage crew: The people who, during a performance, are in charge of changing and setting up the scenery for a play.

stage directions: Instructions that tell actors where and when to move onstage.

stage left: The stage area to an actors' left (not the audience's left)

stage manager: The person who helps the director during rehearsals. He writes down the blocking so that there is a recorded plan of movement, writes up the rehearsal schedule, makes sure the rehearsal space is set up for rehearsals, checks all the lighting and sound equipment to make sure it's in working order, and makes certain that anything the actors and director need is available. He also directs the technical people backstage during a performance.

stage right: The stage area to an actors' right (not the audience's right).

taking focus: When an actor is speaking or moving, she does it boldly and clearly to grab the audience's attention.

understudy: An actor who learns specific parts in a play to be able to substitute for an actor in case he cannot perform.

upstage: The area on the stage that is furthest from the audience.

upstaging: When an actor is blocking another actor so that the audience cannot see her.

"who," "what," and "where": The three necessary ingredients to build a scene.

Suggested Plays and Stories for Kids

PUPPET SHOWS

Plays Children Love: A Treasury of Contemporary and Classic Plays for Children by Coleman A. Jennings and Aurand Harris (Doubleday and Company, Inc.)

Puppet Plays for Special Days by Eleanor Boylan (New Plays, Inc.)

Puppet Plays from Favorite Stories by Lewis Mahlmann and David Cadwalader Jones (Plays, Inc.)

Puppet Shows Using Poems and Stories by Laura Ross (Lothrop, Lee, and Shepard Company)

PLAYS FOR YOUNG CHILDREN

Just So Stories, adapted by Brenda Joyce Dubay, from the book by Rudyard Kipling (I. E. Clark)

"Pinocchio and the Fire Eater" by Aurand Harris, in *Plays Children Love: A Treasury of Contemporary and Classic Plays for Children* (Doubleday)

"Winnie the Pooh," adapted by Kristin Sergel, from the book by A. A. Milne, in *Plays Children Love: A Treasury of Contemporary and Classic Plays for Children* (Doubleday)

MUSICALS

Free to Be You and Me by Marlo Thomas (Bantam Books)

Really Rosie by Maurice Sendak and Carol King (Samuel French)

You're a Good Man, Charlie Brown by Clark Gesner, based on the comic strip by Charles M. Schulz (Random House)

CLASSICS

The Doctor in Spite of Himself, adapted by Bernard Hewitt, from the play by Molière (Baker's Plays)

"The Importance of Being Earnest" by Oscar Wilde, in *Eight Great Comedies* (Mentor Books, New American Library of World Literature)

Midsummer Night's Dream by William Shakespeare

DRAMAS

The Diary of Anne Frank by Frances Goodrich and Albert Hackett (Dramatists Play Service)

The Miracle Worker by William Gibson (Baker's Plays)

The Night Thoreau Spent in Jail by Jerome Lawrence and Robert E. Lee (Samuel French)

Of Mice and Men by John Steinbeck (Dramatists Play Service)

STORIES YOU CAN ADAPT INTO PLAYS

Tales of Hans Christian Anderson

Tales of the Brothers Grimm

Any of your favorite books and stories

Bibliography

Barnet, Sylvan, Morton Berman, and William Burto, editors. *Eight Great Comedies*. New York: Mentor Books, New American Library of World Literature, 1958.

Bellville, Cheryl Walsh. *Theater Magic: Behind the Scenes at a Children's Theater*. Minneapolis, MN: Carolrhoda Books, 1986.

Corey, Melinda, and George Ochoa. *Movie and TV: The New York Public Library Book of Answers*. New York: Stonesong Press, 1992.

Fink, Bert. *Rodgers and Hammerstein Birthday Book*. New York: Abrams, 1993.

Fricke, John, Jay Scarfone, and William Stillman. *The Wizard of Oz: The Official 50th Anniversary Pictoral History*. New York: Warner Books, 1989.

Hay, Peter. *Movie Anecdotes*. New York: Oxford University Press, 1990.

Gassner, John, editor. *Twenty Best Plays of the Modern American Theatre*. New York: Crown Publishers, 1939.

Jennings, Coleman A., and Aurand Harris. *Plays Children Love: A Treasury of Contemporary and Classic Plays for Children*. Garden City, New York: Doubleday, 1981.

Loxton, Howard. *The Arts: Theater*. Austin, TX: Steck-Vaughn Library, 1989.

Morley, Jacqueline, and John James. *Inside Story: Shakespeare's Theater*. New York: Peter Bedrick Books, 1994.

Novelly, Maria C. *Theatre Games for Young Performers: Improvisation and Exercises for Developing Acting Skills*. Colorado Springs, CO: Meriwether Publishers, 1985.

Priestly, J. B. *The Wonderful World of the Theatre*. New York: Rathbone Books, 1959.

Rasmussen, Bruun, and Grete Peterson. *Make-up, Costumes, and Masks*. London: Oak Tree Press, 1976.

Rebello, Stephen. *The Art of Pocahontas*. New York: Hyperion, Welcome Enterprises, and the Walt Disney Company, 1995.

Robertson, Patrick. *The Guinness Book of Movie Facts and Feats*. New York: Abbeville Press Publishers, 1994.

Shakespeare, William. *The Illustrated Stratford Shakespeare*. London: Chancellor Press, 1987.

Sitarz, Paula Gaj. *The Curtain Rises: A History of Theater from Its Origins in Greece and Rome Through the English Restoration*. White Hall, VA: Shoe Tree Press, 1991.

Spolin, Viola. *Improvisation for the Theater*. Evanston, IL: Northwestern University Press, 1963.

Spolin, Viola. *Theater Games for Rehearsal: A Director's Handbook*. Evanston, IL: Northwestern University Press, 1985.

Spolin, Viola. *Theater Games for the Classroom: A Teacher's Handbook*. Evanston, IL: Northwestern University Press, 1986.

Thane, Adele. *Plays from Famous Stories and Fairy Tales: Royalty-Free Dramatizations of Favorite Children's Stories*. Boston: Plays, Inc., 1967.

About the Author

Lisa Bany-Winters began performing in community plays at the age of 11. As much as she loved every aspect of theater, her favorite part was the theater games and improvisation. She founded Emanon Theater Company when she was 15 years old and began directing children's productions based on improvisation. Within eight years, Emanon became an established professional theater company with a talented ensemble of actors. Under Lisa's direction, they created original adaptations of children's classics through improvisation.

In 2007 Lisa cofounded Play On, an educational theater company dedicated to providing professionally implemented, quality theater training in a creative and nurturing environment. Play On focuses on development of the student as an individual, an artist, and an ensemble member. Through Play On, Lisa and her cofounder, Josh Andrews, direct drama camp, children's productions, drama clubs, a kids' comedy team called Code Red Vines, and an adult comedy team called Mouth to Mouth. Play On is primarily located in Evanston, Illinois, and its website is www.playonltd.com.

Lisa's other books include *Show Time*, *Funny Bones*, and *Family Fun Nights*. A graduate of Columbia College, she is currently on the faculty of the Second City, where she teaches improv to adults and children. She and her family live in Glenview, Illinois.

Family Fun Nights
140 Activities the Whole Family Will Enjoy

978-1-55652-608-4

$14.95 (CAN $20.95)

Also available in e-book formats

Packed with imaginative activities to bring the family together and create lifelong memories, *Family Fun Nights: 140 Activities the Whole Family Will Enjoy* is full of ideas that require little or no preparation and use materials that are easily found around the house. The 26 themed family events and related home-based exercises go beyond game night and movie night by creating family traditions that kids will remember and look forward to repeating. Families laugh together on "Giggle Night" and "Opposite Night," explore the world during "Animal Night" and "Science Night," or scare themselves silly on "Spooky Night" and "Mystery Night." Everything parents or grandparents need to make the evening complete is detailed, including skits, songs, crafts, games, and recipes.

CHICAGO
REVIEW
PRESS

Available at your favorite bookstore, (800) 888-4741, or www.chicagoreviewpress.com

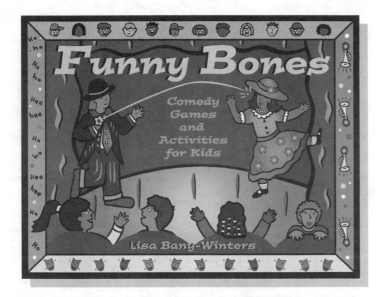

Funny Bones
Comedy Games and Activities for Kids

978-1-55652-444-8
$16.95 (CAN $18.95)
Also available in e-book formats

Kids love to be funny! Every classroom or neighborhood has a kid whose greatest ambition is to make people laugh—and all kids love to laugh at the jokes and antics of their friends. *Funny Bones: Comedy Games and Activities for Kids* boasts 90 amusing activities designed to tickle the funny bone and bring out the humor in every kid. For shy children, the hilarious improvisational games and comedic scenes boost self-confidence and a sense of fun. *Funny Bones* is a great way to bring humor into the classroom and laughter into the home.

Show Time!
Music, Dance, and Drama Activities for Kids

978-1-55652-361-8
$14.95 (CAN $16.95)
Also available in e-book formats

With *Show Time! Music, Dance, and Drama Activities for Kids,* readers will learn to become "triple threat" performers, developing their skills as singers, dancers, and actors. More than 80 activities show kids how to be rising stars—they'll discover how to imitate a musician or musical instrument, act out a song, create a mirror dance, and make puppets and playbills. Along the way, they'll read about the history of musicals and find out how to get it all together before the curtain goes up. *Show Time!* is perfect for teachers who need to prepare performers for a show; for parents who crave fun ways to fill spare minutes with their kids at home, in the car, or in a doctor's waiting room; and for kids who want to enjoy themselves on their own or in a small group.

CHICAGO REVIEW PRESS

Available at your favorite bookstore, (800) 888-4741, or www.chicagoreviewpress.com